MARK ROSENBLATT

Mark Rosenblatt is a writer and director for theatre and screen.

Giant is his first play. It opened at the Royal Court Jerwood Theatre Downstairs in 2024 and won the 2025 Olivier and Critics' Circle Awards for Best New Play. Mark also received the 2025 Critics' Circle Award for Most Promising Playwright.

Previously, he was Associate Director at Leeds Playhouse from 2013 to 2016 and Associate Artist there until 2020. He was Studio Associate at the National Theatre from 2011 to 2013, founded Dumbfounded Theatre in 2001 and won the JMK Award for Directors in 1999.

His extensive directing work includes productions at Shakespeare's Globe, the Young Vic, the National Theatre, Leeds, Sheffield and Northampton Theatres, as well as in New York, LA and Tokyo.

His film work includes the Oscar-longlisted short film *Ganef* (writer-director) and the feature film *Making Noise Quietly* (co-writer).

Other Titles in this Series

Mike Bartlett
THE 47TH
ALBION
BULL
GAME
AN INTERVENTION
KING CHARLES III
MIKE BARTLETT PLAYS: TWO
MRS DELGADO
SCANDALTOWN
SNOWFLAKE
UNICORN
VASSA *after* Gorky
WILD

Chris Bush
THE ASSASSINATION OF KATIE HOPKINS
  with Matt Winkworth
THE CHANGING ROOM
CHRIS BUSH PLAYS: ONE
A DOLL'S HOUSE *after* Ibsen
FAUSTUS: THAT DAMNED WOMAN
HUNGRY
JANE EYRE *after* Brontë
THE LAST NOËL
OTHERLAND
ROBIN HOOD AND THE
  CHRISTMAS HEIST
  with Matt Winkworth
ROCK / PAPER / SCISSORS
STANDING AT THE SKY'S EDGE
  with Richard Hawley
STEEL

Jez Butterworth
THE FERRYMAN
THE HILLS OF CALIFORNIA
JERUSALEM
JEZ BUTTERWORTH PLAYS: ONE
JEZ BUTTERWORTH PLAYS: TWO
MOJO
THE NIGHT HERON
PARLOUR SONG
THE RIVER
THE WINTERLING

Caryl Churchill
BLUE HEART
CHURCHILL PLAYS: THREE
CHURCHILL PLAYS: FOUR
CHURCHILL PLAYS: FIVE
CHURCHILL: SHORTS
CLOUD NINE
DING DONG THE WICKED
A DREAM PLAY *after* Strindberg
DRUNK ENOUGH TO SAY I LOVE YOU?
ESCAPED ALONE
FAR AWAY
GLASS. KILL. BLUEBEARD'S FRIENDS.
  IMP.
HERE WE GO
HOTEL
ICECREAM
LIGHT SHINING IN
  BUCKINGHAMSHIRE
LOVE AND INFORMATION
MAD FOREST
A NUMBER
PIGS AND DOGS
SEVEN JEWISH CHILDREN
THE SKRIKER
THIS IS A CHAIR
THYESTES *after* Seneca
TRAPS
WHAT IF IF ONLY

Natasha Gordon
NINE NIGHT

Lucy Kirkwood
BEAUTY AND THE BEAST
  with Katie Mitchell
BLOODY WIMMIN
THE CHILDREN
CHIMERICA
HEDDA *after* Ibsen
THE HUMAN BODY
IT FELT EMPTY WHEN THE HEART
  WENT AT FIRST BUT IT IS
  ALRIGHT NOW
LUCY KIRKWOOD PLAYS: ONE
MOSQUITOES
NSFW
RAPTURE
TINDERBOX
THE WELKIN

Conor McPherson
THE BRIGHTENING AIR
COLD WAR *after* Paweł Pawlikowski
DUBLIN CAROL
GIRL FROM THE NORTH COUNTRY
  with Bob Dylan
McPHERSON PLAYS: ONE
McPHERSON PLAYS: TWO
McPHERSON PLAYS: THREE
THE NEST *after* Franz Xaver Kroetz
THE NIGHT ALIVE
PORT AUTHORITY
THE SEAFARER
SHINING CITY
UNCLE VANYA *after* Chekhov
THE VEIL
THE WEIR

Jack Thorne
2ND MAY 1997
AFTER LIFE *after* Hirokazu Kore-eda
BUNNY
BURYING YOUR BROTHER IN
  THE PAVEMENT
A CHRISTMAS CAROL *after* Dickens
THE END OF HISTORY…
HOPE
JACK THORNE PLAYS: ONE
JACK THORNE PLAYS: TWO
JUNKYARD
LET THE RIGHT ONE IN
  after John Ajvide Lindqvist
THE MOTIVE AND THE CUE
MYDIDAE
THE SOLID LIFE OF SUGAR WATER
STACY & FANNY AND FAGGOT
WHEN YOU CURE ME
WHEN WINSTON WENT TO WAR WITH
  THE WIRELESS
WOYZECK *after* Büchner

debbie tucker green
BORN BAD
DEBBIE TUCKER GREEN PLAYS: ONE
DIRTY BUTTERFLY
EAR FOR EYE
HANG
NUT
A PROFOUNDLY AFFECTIONATE,
  PASSIONATE DEVOTION TO
  SOMEONE (– *NOUN*)
RANDOM
STONING MARY
TRADE & GENERATIONS
TRUTH AND RECONCILIATION

Mark Rosenblatt

GIANT

NICK HERN BOOKS
London
www.nickhernbooks.co.uk

A Nick Hern Book

Giant first published in Great Britain in 2024 as a paperback original by Nick Hern Books Limited, The Glasshouse, 49a Goldhawk Road, London W12 8QP

Reprinted in this revised edition with a new cover in 2025

Giant copyright © 2024, 2025 Mark Rosenblatt

Mark Rosenblatt has asserted his moral right to be identified as the author of this work

Cover artwork: AKA

Designed and typeset by Nick Hern Books, London
Printed in the UK by by Mimeo Ltd

A CIP catalogue record for this book is available from the British Library

ISBN 978 1 83904 443 4

CAUTION All rights whatsoever in this play are strictly reserved. Requests to reproduce the texts in whole or in part should be addressed to the publisher.

Amateur Performing Rights Applications for performance, including readings and excerpts, by amateurs in the English language throughout the world should be addressed to the Performing Rights Manager, Nick Hern Books, The Glasshouse, 49a Goldhawk Road, London W12 8QP, *tel* +44 (0)20 8749 4953, *email* rights@nickhernbooks.co.uk, except as follows:

Australia: ORiGiN Theatrical, *email* enquiries@originmusic.com.au, *web* www.origintheatrical.com.au

New Zealand: Play Bureau, 20 Rua Street, Mangapapa, Gisborne, 4010, *tel* +64 21 258 3998, *email* info@playbureau.com

United States of America and Canada: The Agency (London) Ltd, see details below

Professional Performing Rights Applications for performance by professionals in any medium and in any language throughout the world (and amateur and stock performances in the United States of America and Canada) should be addressed to The Agency (London) Ltd, 24 Pottery Lane, Holland Park, London W11 4LZ, *fax* +44 (0)20 7727 9037, *email* info@theagency.co.uk

No performance of any kind may be given unless a licence has been obtained. Applications should be made before rehearsals begin. Publication of this play does not necessarily indicate its availability for amateur performance.

www.nickhernbooks.co.uk/environmental-policy

Nick Hern Books' authorised representative in the EU is Easy Access System Europe – Mustamäe tee 50, 10621 Tallinn, Estonia
email gpsr.requests@easproject.com

Giant was first performed at the Royal Court Jerwood Theatre Downstairs, London, on 20 September 2024. The cast was as follows:

ROALD DAHL	John Lithgow
TOM MASCHLER	Elliot Levey
FELICITY 'LICCY' CROSLAND	Rachael Stirling
HALLIE	Tessa Bonham Jones
JESSIE STONE	Romola Garai
WALLY SAUNDERS	Richard Hope

Director	Nicholas Hytner
Designer	Bob Crowley
Lighting Designer	Anna Watson
Sound Designer	Alexandra Faye Braithwaite
Casting Director	Arthur Carrington
Associate Designer	Jaimie Todd
Assistant Director	Bellaray Bertrand-Webb
Props Supervisor	Lily Mollgaard
Dialect	Hazel Holder
Hair, Wigs & Make-Up	Campbell Young Associates
Stage Manager	Laura Hammond
Deputy Stage Manager	Andrew McCarthy
Assistant Stage Manager	Zoë Gledhill
Sound Operator	Patrick O'Sullivan
Costume Alterations	Anna Barcock
Dresser	Adam Rainer

Giant transferred to the Harold Pinter Theatre in London's West End on 26 April 2025, produced by Brian and Dayna Lee, Stephanie Kramer, Nicole Kramer, Josh Fiedler, Robyn Goodman, and the Royal Court Theatre, with the following change to the cast:

JESSIE STONE	Aya Cash

Author's Note

The summer of 1983 was a particularly challenging season to be (or be near) Roald Dahl. Newly divorced from his wife of thirty years, freshly engaged to his mistress of eleven, in physical agony, unsettled by the renovation of his family home, racing to ready his latest book for publication, and vilified in the press for a book review he himself deemed righteous and heroic. All the biographies, related books, articles, my own conversations with journalists who interviewed him that summer, paint the same picture – of a ferociously driven, capricious children's author in a moment of great upheaval.

My play *Giant* riffs on all this, blending these very real circumstances with a dramatic encounter I have entirely imagined. That, on one of those summer afternoons in 1983, Roald Dahl's British and American publishers visited him at home to encourage him to make an apology and help restore his damaged reputation.

If my research missed it, and something like this *did* happen in reality, it could never have played out as it does in *Giant*. For whilst Tom Maschler was indeed Roald's UK publisher at this time, his US counterpart in the play never existed. Her employer – Farrar, Straus and Giroux – *was* Roald's US publisher, but Jessie Stone is my invention alone and, as the old saying goes, any resemblance to any persons living or dead is entirely coincidental.

Giant is a hybrid of the real and imagined, hopefully catching the spirit of a moment in time, but never striving to be documentary. There is one thing in *Giant*, however, which is purely Roald Dahl's. When you hear his book review quoted, they are his actual words. And, later in the play, when he communicates further with the outside world, those are his words too, though I have reorganised and amalgamated them from several sources. In the midst of my conjuring of Dahl's private world that summer, sit his unvarnished public utterances. They belong to the real Roald Dahl's complex legacy.

M.R.

To A, L & R

*And to all the playwrights I've worked with and admired
for showing me what a play can be*

Characters

ROALD DAHL, *sixty-seven, famous children's author*
FELICITY 'LICCY' CROSLAND, *forty-five, Roald's fiancée, a successful interior designer*
TOM MASCHLER, *forty-nine, managing director of Jonathan Cape, Roald's British publisher*
JESSIE STONE, *mid-thirties, sales director at Farrar, Straus and Giroux, Roald's American publisher*
HALLIE, *twenty-six, Gipsy House's New Zealander cook and housekeeper*
WALLY SAUNDERS, *seventy-four, Roald's handyman, builder and all-round ancient retainer*

The voice of MIKE COREN, *twenties,* New Statesman *reporter*

Note on Text

/ means overlapping dialogue. Occasional.

… means a trailing thought or fading intention.

'–' is a cut-off, interrupted speech.

Note on Play

The action of the play takes place in (almost) real time across an afternoon in the early summer of 1983 at Gipsy House, Roald Dahl's long-standing family home in Great Missenden, Buckinghamshire, England.

This text went to press before the end of rehearsals and so may differ slightly from the play as performed.

ACT ONE

The sitting room at Gipsy House, Great Missenden, Roald Dahl's long-time family home. The house is having a major refurbishment and, despite a creeping infestation of dust sheets and floor protectors, this room is the last sanctuary from dust and works. Roald's art has been boxed and stacked against skirting boards, blending into a larger pile of storage boxes, each carefully labelled and piled against one wall. Some furniture is dust-sheeted, whilst other pieces – the odd chair, a side-table with a telephone on it – are still in use. A doorway leads to the hall, another to the kitchen, whilst the French windows leading to the garden have been removed, replaced by polythene builders' sheets. If we could see into the garden, we'd see an expanse of rich green, a cottage garden, a tunnel of lime trees leading to Roald's writing shed, a large gypsy caravan beyond it, then fields and hedgerows.

It's the summer of 1983. One of those hot, stifling, hazy days. ROALD DAHL (sixty-seven years old and 6-foot-4) sits in the middle of the room, at a table half-set for lunch, proofing a document. When he speaks, there's something un-English that offsets his posh voice. When he moves, it's through a cacophony of pain. With him is TOM MASCHLER, forty-nine, a dark-haired, olive-skinned, Jewish man, a mix, on appearance, of Ashkenazi and Sephardi heritage, primed for a game of tennis. When he speaks, he's loud, certain, not posh, hard to place.

They're inspecting a book. ROALD stares at it intently, as if at a glistening diamond.

ROALD. Yes, yes.

TOM. Yes?

ROALD. Yes.

Pause.

He's finally cracked them.

TOM. Good.

ROALD. Much nastier. Blistering scalps, clawed fingers, good. And her in the middle. Relishing the bloodlust to come. Good boy, Quentin.

ROALD *turns through the pages, utterly lost in the proof, occasionally leaning in. Eventually:*

TOM. I've got a terrific idea about the other thing – bit of a silver bullet –

ROALD *laughs at something in the proof.*

ROALD. That's very good. Pencil?

TOM. Oh.

TOM *reaches into his pocket, hands him one.*

(*Tries again.*) 'Cause we should do *something* –

ROALD. No no no no!

TOM. What?

ROALD. Why's she *there*? The eye pulls to it *before* the boy talks about the tree.

TOM. Mark it, we'll deal with it.

ROALD. If the bloody witch is there before he's said it there's simply no surprise!

TOM. Mark it.

ROALD. But I don't want to just mark it and then wait until it's done before I see it again. Do you understand? I know you –

TOM. What?

ROALD. – you'll move it a tiddly bit in as a sop to me and then it'll be too late for anything more. What pencil is this? It's like writing with an ice cream. I want it to move there, to the bottom or even the next page – (*He flips to the next page and back again, reconsiders.*) no, to the bottom here. Then bump this up, yes? Otherwise it's for nothing. All the work. May as well just be a bloody picture book by Quentin Blake –

TOM. We'll bike you the adjustments.

ROALD. With additional text by an angry Norwegian. How much is Quentin on again?

TOM. We – no, no –

ROALD. I want to hear you say it.

TOM. – this is done, Roald.

ROALD. So I know I'm not going mad.

TOM. The madness is not / *this*.

ROALD. I do all this conjuring –

TOM. It's all fair and proper –

ROALD. – plot and jokes –

TOM. – legally binding –

ROALD. – hunched over in that –

TOM. – thank *god*.

ROALD. – bloody shed, pulling it out my arse, seven days a week, for an entire year. And then in flutters the Sidcup Cherub and swoops off with half my royalties.

TOM. Not half.

ROALD. For a few misplaced drawings.

TOM (*warning*). *Roald*. Every illustrator shares royalties –

ROALD. But half?

TOM. Not half.

ROALD. Then how much?

Suddenly a bang from upstairs. It goes straight through ROALD*'s upper body.*

Christ!

TOM. Alright?

More bangs. ROALD *flinches*.

ROALD. It's like they're scaling my fucking spine.

TOM. Why not rent somewhere till it's done?

ROALD. Little demons with little ice picks.

TOM. I saw cottages to rent in the next village.

ROALD. I don't fit in cottages.

TOM. You do know you're not *actually* a giant.

ROALD. I'm not not one either.

> LICCY *comes in from upstairs carrying a large box and stacks it on the pile against the wall.* ROALD *winces again, stretches.*

What's happening up there?

LICCY. Test punch-through.

ROALD. They must be careful.

LICCY. Always. They'll stop as soon as the American arrives.

ROALD. Why can't they stop when *I* arrive?

LICCY. Are you going to be like this all day?

ROALD. What? Sentient?

LICCY. Bill's got an hour now, then he's on my Fulham job till next week. Here, let me…

> LICCY *comes over, rubs his shoulders; he half-resists, then, groaning at her touch, succumbs.*
>
> *She spies the proofs.*

Ooh, they look *horrid*. Quent's so very clever, isn't he?

ROALD. He's single, Lis, move in with him.

> …*and* LICCY *leans across, peers in at the proof, then laughs.*

LICCY. Living with someone nice, what a fun idea. (*Of the page.*) *I love* her nasty itchy head. Ooh.

ROALD. How old did this American sound?

LICCY. I don't know. Rushed call, busy station.

ROALD (*tart*). A hundred?

LICCY. Late twenties, thirties, possibly.

ACT ONE   13

ROALD. A child. They always send me children.

TOM. Young, old, shows Roger cares.

ROALD. It's true!

TOM. Did she give any sense of timings? Because I can't hang about.

ROALD. Just because I write about them doesn't mean I have to be managed by them. Last week, little chap turned up – remember him, Lis? – must have been about ten. Sweet boy. I was about to look for his football in the garden when he said he'd come to interview me for the BBC.

TOM *laughs.*

Bet they don't send Kingsley Amis children. Bet Kingsley is sent the sage and the wise. Bet Sir Kingsley gets the bloody prime minister. (*To* LICCY, *wanting her gone.*) Please, darling Lis.

LICCY. Right, sorry.

She takes a step back. ROALD *tries to re-engage with the proof but her presence impedes. Flicks back at her.*

What?

ROALD. Shoo.

LICCY. Don't shoo me. Can I not just... hover?

ROALD. No.

LICCY. You won't notice me.

ROALD. But I very much am. And I have to get this done.

LICCY. Look, I'm slender and invisible. It's like having a fairy in the room. A lovely, slightly humiliated fairy.

ROALD *stares at her.* LICCY, *embarrassed, rearranges her pride. She pours a glass of lemonade from the jug.*

Right, well I'll go and refresh Constable Dunn then. Go where I'm appreciated.

TOM. How long will he be there? Outside?

ROALD. Worried about getting your throat slit?

LICCY. Until the calls stop. Or they catch the bastard.

TOM (*to* ROALD). We *have* to take you out the phone book.

ROALD. Never!

TOM. Liccy, tell him.

LICCY. He doesn't want my help.

And she's gone out into the hall. A beat.

TOM. Roald, it's madness. Let my office deal with your fan mail.

ROALD. No no no. I need them to write to *me*. Here.

TOM. But they will.

ROALD. They won't if it's care-of snory-bory London office.

TOM. Half Cape's authors are care-of.

ROALD. The *children* won't write to a publishing house, Tom. And I can't risk it. And this madman isn't going to ruin that.

TOM. Just for six months?

ROALD. End of memo.

He settles back into the proof. TOM *gets up, takes a little foray round the room, looks at the boxes. To loosen up, he mimes a swing of a tennis racket – a dynamic backhand.*

Are you ever not playing tennis?

TOM. Championship point up here. Always.

ROALD. And who are you vanquishing today?

TOM. Ian McEwan at three o'clock. If he plays like he writes, I'm fucked.

He smashes an imaginary tramline volley, a brief McEnroe-esque air-punch.

ROALD. We don't need your protection, Captain Big Balls. I know the difference between a late-night crank call and actual proper danger.

TOM. *How?* How do you *know* he's harmless?

ROALD *holds back what he wants to say.*

ACT ONE   15

ROALD. *Because*.

TOM. Because?

ROALD. Yes.

Beat.

TOM. What did he actually say?

ROALD (*with relish*). At the end – right at the end – after lots of maniacal blather, he said – terribly good image, actually – he said he wanted to be arrested soaked in our blood.

TOM. Christ.

ROALD. Poop more like.

TOM. How do you know?!

ROALD. Genuinely violent people don't call ahead.

TOM. Don't say that to the IRA.

ROALD. He's a loner. A bitter bloody loner from Stamford Hill. Or Golders Green or Hendon or wherever your chaps tend to live nowadays.

TOM. Kensington?

ROALD. Forgive me, yes. I'll have the Met put you top of the suspect list. You do so love making phone calls.

TOM. Bang to rights.

ROALD. I *knew* it! (*Calls.*) Officer! A confession!

ROALD puts down the pencil.

I will not start caring-of because of him. I will not start anything because of him. Now can we *please* stop yabbering and – ?

A massive, jolting bang-crash upstairs.

Fuck! Liccy! It's *impossible*!

LICCY (*off, downstairs*). I'll go, stay there – (*Calls.*) Bill!

LICCY's footsteps up the stairs.

ROALD. Unbearable.

LICCY (*upstairs*). Bill!

TOM. Take it to your hut.

ROALD. Wally's doused the bloody lawn in pesticide. We'll suffocate before we get past the flowerbeds. Honestly, it's *Escape from Colditz*. Everywhere I turn.

A heavy drag across the floor upstairs.

(*Calls.*) Hallie! What are we eating?

HALLIE (*off, New Zealand accent*). Salad Niçoise.

ROALD. Sancerre or Chablis, Tom?

TOM. Chablis.

ROALD. Correct.

TOM. But don't open it for me.

ROALD. I'm very much not.

ROALD *gets up stiffly – and as he reaches full height we realise how small he makes the room feel, like an ancient giraffe rallying itself to feed.*

LICCY (*calls down*). It's done, they've stopped, it's finished. Okay?

ROALD (*calls, sharp, loud*). They damage anything?

Beat. Nothing.

(*Calls again.*) They bloody damage anything, Lis?

Beat. Quick footsteps on the stairs and LICCY *appears in the doorway.*

LICCY (*embarrassed, hushed*). No. No. They're looking after everything. I *promise*.

ROALD. They'd better not. (*Calls up.*) You'd better not!

LICCY (*seething*). It's my own firm, in my own home.

ROALD. But it's *her* room!

LICCY. I know, I know!

ACT ONE   17

ROALD. They need to take care!

LICCY winces and ROALD, *sensing her frustration and his excess, holds her arms tenderly, looks her in the eyes, kisses her.*

Sorry. Sorry.

LICCY. Just – *calm*.

ROALD. Yes yes.

LICCY. Gentle.

ROALD. Yes yes.

LICCY. *Gentle*.

ROALD. Yes. Glass of something?

LICCY (*softened*). Yes. Please. I'll go, you work.

ROALD. No no. Done for now.

LICCY. Sure?

ROALD. Yes yes.

As he ambles out the door into the hall:

LICCY. Let Hallie help you.

ROALD. I. Will. Be. Fine.

LICCY (*calls*). Hallie, help Mr Dahl.

ROALD. I. Will. Be. Tickety. Boo.

LICCY and TOM alone. An out-breath.

LICCY. Sorry.

TOM. No no.

LICCY. He's –

TOM. It's really fine.

LICCY starts to ready the table.

Huge adjustment, isn't it?

LICCY (*conceding*). Mammoth. (*Hushed, stressed.*) But he's *soooo* – I've never seen him like this… not just the dust, everything –

TOM. And it's going to be *spectacular.*

LICCY. Is it?

TOM. Yes! Really. Such a long old road.

LICCY. And winding.

TOM. And you're *here*.

LICCY. And some nasty hairpin beds. And dark bloody terrifying forests. But yes, I'm here –

TOM. You're here.

LICCY. We're here. I know.

TOM. Hooray.

LICCY. Thank you, dear man.

TOM. It's done.

LICCY. When Pat collected her things last week, I felt so –

TOM. You've *got* to get on and enjoy it.

LICCY (*ruefully*). I know, I know. And we were. Just. We were. And then he goes and does *this*.

Beat.

TOM. We can make it go away. Or at least stink less.

LICCY. So much stink, Tom.

TOM. Whiff, more a whiff.

LICCY. You saw that hideous thing yesterday in the *Spectator*?

TOM. Of course.

LICCY. '*The most disgraceful thing*' –

TOM. He's –

LICCY. – '*to be written in the English language*' –

TOM. Okay –

ACT ONE   19

LICCY. – '*for a very long time.*'

TOM (*laughs*). He's, Paul Johnson's a total hysteric.

LICCY. It's *everywhere*, Tom. Not just Johnson. All the rags. Left and right. Class and muck. Friend of mine rang yesterday to say bloody *Time Out* are *re*publishing it.

TOM. In *support*.

LICCY (*incredulous*). Protest, support. My god, he wrote a book review, not an Act of fucking Parliament.

TOM. Wasn't your bog-standard book review. Israel, isn't it? Bloody hornets' nest.

LICCY. I know.

TOM. Poke at your peril. Especially if querying its very existence.

LICCY (*rueful*). Oh to be back in the deep dark dark of the deep dark forests.

TOM. Liccy –

LICCY. Honestly!

TOM (*hushed*). – he just needs to say something publicly. However small.

LICCY. Yes, yes.

TOM. Then we can use it. Then it's gone.

LICCY. Like that?

TOM. Like that.

LICCY. I don't believe in magic.

From the cellar, semi-audible:

ROALD (*off*). Hallie! Torch!

LICCY. Christ. (*Calls.*) Hallie, help Mr Dahl please!

HALLIE (*off*). I am!

LICCY (*calls*). Roald. Accept the help, please! (*Quicker.*) And the American? Who is she?

TOM. FSG executive.

LICCY. I know that but –

TOM. Sales. Someone Roger trusts.

LICCY. Roald thinks it's a total waste of time. That we're all up to something.

TOM. Well we are. And this girl will help us. She'll give him proper context about the *Witches* campaign out there. I'll do the same, gently, from our end. And then I'll skedaddle.

LICCY. And you've briefed her?

TOM. When? She landed at six a.m.

LICCY (*anxious*). On the phone, I don't know. She needs briefing.

TOM. Look, she's late, Liccy, sure, not great, but she won't crash in here in clown shoes. She's one of Roger's lot. Sharp, smart, *Manhattanista*. She'll know what he can be like.

LICCY. I hope you're right. I'm –

ROALD (*offstage*)....Got it!

The sound of ROALD *approaching, bottles jangling.*

LICCY. – and it's glorious you came all this way too. And he appreciates it too – even if he doesn't know it yet.

ROALD, *lit cigarette in mouth, enters brandishing a bottle of Chablis and a corkscrew. He puts them down, starts opening the wine.*

ROALD. Appreciates what?

LICCY. Sugar and spice.

ROALD (*stagily suspicious*). Hmmm. No spilling state secrets, Liccy. He looks friendly, but he's a snake.

TOM. We were talking about the house.

ROALD. Didn't sound like it.

TOM. I hadn't realised quite how much you were doing.

ROALD. Ah yes. Liccy's grand vision.

LICCY. I've been boring him with the room by room.

ROALD. Fibbers.

LICCY. I have.

ROALD. Terrible terrible fibblers.

TOM. Don't set for me, I'll zip off once –

LICCY. You can sit with us, you're not seven.

Cork pops.

ROALD (*smells the wine*). I have five hundred of these bastards. Bloke in Speen does a Calais run twice a year – white-van job. Better be bloody yummy, otherwise I'm stuck with a vast stash of grim grape.

He pours three glasses, hands to TOM *and* LICCY.

TOM. Just a touch.

ROALD. Have a fucking glass.

TOM. Thanks.

ROALD. McEwan can bloody wait.

TOM. Toast?

LICCY. Why not?

ROALD (*of wine*). Good colour at least.

TOM. To a new life in a new home.

LICCY. Thank you, Tom.

ROALD. Thank you, Schmoozy.

LICCY. He's being a darling, darling.

ROALD. He wants something, Lis.

TOM. Yes, joy and love. And – do you know – and I hate bullshit –

ROALD. Ha!

TOM. I do!

ROALD. Such a bootlicker!

TOM. – but I really, really can't think of a couple who love each other the way you do.

ROALD. The Mighty Spootlicker!

TOM (*insistent*). Really!

LICCY. Apart from today.

TOM. *Especially* today. All this and you're still in the same room.

ROALD. Only one we can be in.

LICCY. A dream, a dream!

TOM. But it is! In a way, it *is*!

ROALD. The Mightiest Spootlicker.

TOM. And all this crap will pass and you'll both be out there, on the lawn, in the sun, a book, some more of this –

ROALD. Needs to breathe, but sod it –

TOM. – and your greatest adventure can truly begin.

LICCY squeezes ROALD's *hand with great affection.*

ROALD. Can we bloody drink now?

LICCY. To the passing of crap.

ROALD. To passing crap.

TOM. To *love* hard-earned.

She kisses ROALD.

ROALD (*coy*). Beh.

LICCY. Idiot.

They drink. ROALD *pulls her into him slightly. A tender connection.*

TOM (*of the wine*). Ooh –

ROALD. What?

ACT ONE   23

From the hall, a female American voice:

VOICE (*off, quiet*). Hello?

ROALD. Did I overpay?

TOM. Depends what you paid?

VOICE (*off, louder*). Hello?

They all turn.

LICCY. Oh!

ROALD. The eaglet has landed.

LICCY (*to* ROALD). Sois sage! (*Calls.*) Hello? (*Back to* ROALD.) I'm serious.

LICCY *springs up and goes into the hall.*

ROALD. Fifteen hundred.

TOM. Mmmmmm.

The men listen and, simultaneously:

LICCY (*off*). Hello, do come in, I'm Felicity.

JESSIE. (*off*). Jessie Stone, / hi.

LICCY (*off*). We spoke on the telephone.

ROALD. This only need be brief, okay?

TOM. Absolutely.

JESSIE (*off*). I'm sorry to be so late.

LICCY (*off*). Not at all.

ROALD (*to* TOM). She one of your gang, Tom?

TOM. What?

ROALD. This girl? One of yours?

LICCY, *carrying a light summer coat over her arm, shepherds in* JESSIE STONE – *mid-thirties, poised, East Coast American, white, blonde, a bit out of puff and hot, clutching a bag.*

LICCY. Roald, Mrs Stone. (*Calls*.) Hallie!

ROALD. Hello.

JESSIE. Hello. Jessie Stone. It's an honour.

ROALD. Roald Dahl.

JESSIE. No mistaking you, sir.

ROALD. Why's that?

JESSIE. Because you're –

    ROALD *contorts momentarily into some kind of angular ghoul.*

ROALD (*ghoulish voice*). Very distinctive?

JESSIE. Tall. Familiar. *Very* familiar.

LICCY (*calls*). Hallie!

ROALD (*teasing*). You sound weary of the sight of me.

JESSIE. No, not at all!

ROALD. Phewee, can't have that!

JESSIE. Your photo is on our office wall.

ROALD. I'm a pin-up! Hear that, Lis?

    HALLIE *pops into the doorway – she's twenty-six, a New Zealander, warm, perky, busy.*

HALLIE (*to* LICCY). Hi.

    LICCY *hands her* JESSIE*'s coat.*

JESSIE. I'm really so sorry to be so late.

ROALD. June's Hot Hunk.

LICCY. Simmer, darling.

JESSIE. I got on the wrong train, had to go –

ROALD. Hear that, Hal?

JESSIE. – go back to Paddington to get on the right one.

ROALD (*to* HALLIE). Hunk of the Month.

HALLIE. Just the *month*, Mr D?

JESSIE. I hope I haven't missed anything important.

TOM (*flatly*). No, we've been waiting for you. Tom Maschler.

JESSIE. Of course, Mr Maschler.

LICCY. Sorry! Thoughtless. Stupidly assumed you'd know each other.

JESSIE. I don't normally work closely with senior editorial. One can dream but… they tend to keep us far from Mount Olympus. Delighted to meet you, sir. You're famous in our office too.

ROALD. More famous than me?

JESSIE. Ha, no.

TOM (*mock-shock*). No?

JESSIE (*stumped for an instant, then*). You're both equally and wildly admired.

LICCY. My god, don't indulge these frail and delicate souls any longer. And welcome, welcome to Gipsy House.

JESSIE. It's a great honour to be here.

ROALD. So much honour.

JESSIE. No really. I was – I was raised on your work, Mr Dahl.

ROALD. You ate my books?

HALLIE disappears with JESSIE's coat and returns a moment later.

JESSIE. Yes! Devoured them! *James and the Giant Peach* was my everything when I was eleven! Perched in the linen closet reading it over and over again.

ROALD. Very charming.

JESSIE. True! / So now –

ROALD. Some wine?

JESSIE. No, no thank you, / I'm –

LICCY. She's pooped, darling.

JESSIE. So now, to work on it, on your new one, to visit with you – it's…

ROALD. An honour?

JESSIE. Yes. It *is*. Truly.

ROALD. Most kind.

LICCY. Sit, sit.

ROALD. Yes, yes, unweary yourself.

JESSIE. Thanks, thank you.

She sits.

TOM. Okay, so –

LICCY. And apologies for all this mess.

JESSIE. No, not at all.

LICCY. Big refurb.

ROALD. Aka the Apocalypse.

JESSIE. I saw, even outside. But, yes, quite a project.

LICCY. We're shifting a lot around.

ROALD. Hell and earth.

LICCY. Roald's finding it a little –

ROALD. Apocalyptic.

LICCY. But he never mentions it, so you'd never know.

ROALD. Ha ha.

LICCY. And the lawn's being fumigated, so we're in here, I'm afraid.

ROALD. No escape.

LICCY. And how was your flight? (*To* TOM.) Sit, Tom, sit.

TOM. I'm happy standing.

JESSIE. Uneventful, thank god.

LICCY (*to* JESSIE). When did you land?

JESSIE. Oh, I –

She glances, almost imperceptibly, at TOM.

– around six a.m. But I'm fine so far. My son's an early riser, so the red-eye's basically a vacation.

LICCY. Well, thank you for rushing here.

JESSIE. Of course. And Roger sends his regards. He was really *incredibly* shocked to hear about the press situation and then this awful, horrible police matter. All of us were. And he wants to help however he can.

ROALD. All entirely unnecessary.

LICCY. But very appreciated.

ROALD. Fuss over nothing.

LICCY. Delighted you're here. Lemonade?

JESSIE. Water's just fine.

LICCY *pours some water into a glass.*

LICCY. You must try Hallie's lemonade before you go.

LICCY *gives her the glass.*

JESSIE. Thank you. Are you – ?

LICCY. She makes it fresh and it's really special.

HALLIE (*embarrassed*). Hi. It's just lemonade.

JESSIE. I'm excited to try it. Are the police any clearer about who made the calls?

ROALD. Call.

LICCY. He tried the night before, didn't he?

ROALD. Rang off, terrified.

LICCY. We're told there's some leads.

ROALD. Smorgasbord of nut-nuts.

JESSIE. Horrible.

LICCY. Yes, well.

ROALD. Of course it's my fault.

LICCY. And how old's your boy?

JESSIE. Fifteen next month.

ROALD. Fifteen! You must have been five when you had him!

LICCY. Rude.

ROALD. Praise.

JESSIE. I'm older than you think.

ROALD. You look like a tiddler.

LICCY. Not praise.

ROALD. Old crone in disguise?

LICCY. *Sorry*, Mrs Stone!

JESSIE. No, no, it's –

ROALD. Rip off that radiant face to find beneath –

LICCY. Enough.

ROALD. – an ancient wrinkled monster! A terrible banshee! (*Sudden pivot back to conversational.*) He a fan too? Linen-closet lurker like his mother?

JESSIE. Um, actually, yes. Huge. I read – I've been reading your books to him since he was small. In fact – not now, but at some point –

She reaches into her bag, lifts out a book to show the title.

– I was hoping to get you to, uh, sign this.

TOM. Christ.

JESSIE. He'll kill me if I forget!

ROALD. He's too old for *The Twits*, surely?

JESSIE. Well, no, he – he just loves it, always has –

ROALD. Almost ready for the short stories now.

LICCY. Do *not* let him read the short stories.

ROALD. Why ever not? Sneak preview on the adult mind. He'll find out about us soon enough.

LICCY. They're not for a nice fifteen-year-old boy.

ROALD. Fifteen-year-old boys are generally not nice.

LICCY. Don't listen to him.

ROALD. They're sweaty and pimply and think about muck. Mrs Stone?

JESSIE. Well, Archie's – um –

ROALD. What, a saint? Ha! He's got you swizzled. Cunning devil. Give it here.

JESSIE. Now?

ROALD. Whilst the iron's *sizzling*.

JESSIE. Oh, um –

She takes the book out of her bag, goes to retrieve something from inside it.

ROALD. Got a pen?

JESSIE. Oh –

ROALD. Chop-chop.

She puts the book down and looks in her handbag for one as TOM, *eager to get on, ferries the book over to* ROALD. JESSIE, *a little alarmed by this, fishes out the pen quickly and passes it, via* LICCY, *to* ROALD.

And is there a bit he liked especially?

JESSIE. Oh the beard. All the food and the nest...

ROALD. It's either nesty-beard, the glass eye or little boys' bums. You, Hal?

HALLIE. Oh yeah the bums, Mr D, so funny.

ROALD *opens the book to sign it and a piece of folded paper slides out.*

ROALD. Oops.

JESSIE *looks slightly alarmed.* ROALD's *about to hand it back when he sees what it is.*

Hello hello?

JESSIE. It's just your article, I was –

ROALD *opens it up, looks.*

ROALD. My scandalous book review! And *covered* in scrawly spider scribbles. Cobwebs galore. Are you the spider?

LICCY. Roald, it's her prep, give it back.

He squints, can't read them. Turns the page round to follow one.

JESSIE. My writing is –

ROALD. *Lots* of notes.

TOM. Diligence.

ROALD. Lots and lots and lots. Fiery exclamations everywhere.

LICCY (*sensing jeopardy*). Roald, come on. Not fair.

ROALD. Ooh. *Four* question marks here in an angry huddle. What's this – does that say 'true'? (*Looks again.*) '*Not* true!'? What's not true?

LICCY. All to be discussed, Roald –

ROALD. Strong objections, clearly.

LICCY. – once we've eaten.

ROALD, *still holding the article, looks at an anxious* JESSIE. *Finally, he smiles to himself and folds it up.*

ROALD. Of course, how naughty of me. Racing ahead.

He hands it back to her. She puts it back in her bag. A moment.

Race, race, race. (*Of the autograph.*) Now what was I about to write?

JESSIE. Doesn't have to / be now.

ROALD. No, let's do it before you scarper.

JESSIE. Okay.

ROALD. Get to know you. Better acquainted, better the message, don't you think?

JESSIE. Okay. Wonderful. Thank you.

ROALD. Of course. Delighted.

Uneasy moment.

LICCY. Right. Let's eat. Everyone sit.

TOM. Not for me.

LICCY. Hallie? What deliciousness have you for us?

HALLIE. Oh uh sure it's uh simple really.

Salad Niçoise – and gorgeous beans – just out this morning, Mr Dahl –

ROALD. Very good.

LICCY. It's all from the garden.

HALLIE. And fresh tuna – not from the garden – with a lemon and garlic dressing.

TOM. Lovely.

JESSIE. Wonderful, thank you.

ROALD. Toothbrushes for everyone.

LICCY. Do tuck in – thank you, Hallie –

JESSIE. Thank you. Looks wonderful.

She offers the bread basket to TOM *who takes a piece as* LICCY *goes round to serve* ROALD.

LICCY. Hallie works miracles.

HALLIE. Thank you!

ROALD. Saint Hallie of Auckland!

Raises a little glass to the chef, who does an embarrassed benediction mime…

HALLIE. Um. Bon appétit.

…and sidles off into the kitchen.

TOM. So um Roger sent Mrs Stone here to –

JESSIE. Yes, to make sure someone from FSG was on hand so you felt supported / and informed.

ROALD. So I don't leave, you mean.

JESSIE. Sorry?

LICCY passes the bread along. Beat.

ROALD. Poor Rodge is worried that if he didn't despatch an eager beaver in this time of great distress, I'd get terribly grumpy with him and piss off.

LICCY. Roald!

ROALD. Because he knows I have form. That I leave publishers if I'm not treated properly. He referenced my departure from Knopf, no doubt. Pepper, please. No? Of course he did. Needn't worry – this is different. Entirely.

JESSIE. He just thought it better to discuss this in person. The phone is so...

ROALD. Crackly?

JESSIE. Impersonal.

LICCY. Especially if there's action to take.

ROALD. What kind of action?

LICCY. Well in case they think we ought to say something.

ROALD. Stop prompting, Lis.

LICCY. I'm not.

ROALD. She's doing admirably on her own. What exactly do you do at Farrar Straus Giroux, Mrs Stone?

JESSIE. Oh, did Roger not say?

ROALD. I go rather blank on titles.

JESSIE. I'm a sales director. I work with the sales team. Principally on the children's list. We liaise with all our handsellers, the networks of independents, the chains, the libraries, make sure your books are on all their shelves.

ROALD (*winks*). Desk monkey?

ACT ONE   33

JESSIE. I have a desk, yes.

Beat.

ROALD. And is it your first job?

LICCY. Dearest darling.

ROALD. Is that such a terrible thing to say? You seem terribly young, terribly nervous.

JESSIE. Do I?

ROALD. I thought there might be congratulations in order. I don't want to be rude.

LICCY. His manners are widely celebrated.

Beat.

JESSIE. Well, it's my third. Second at FSG. I came in as an associate, now I'm a director. Before that I was at an agency.

TOM. Roger tells me she's a rising star.

JESSIE. I don't know about that.

ROALD. And are you Jewish?

LICCY. Roald! I'm so sorry –

ROALD. Tom and I were discussing your name –

TOM. Were we?

LICCY. *Please.*

ROALD. – and couldn't quite work it out. Stone? Was that Stein once?

LICCY. No no.

JESSIE. Well, I…

LICCY. Mrs Stone, you really don't have to answer that!

ROALD. Why? Tom is. You wouldn't mind me asking Tom? I just want to know.

LICCY. It's personal. People don't just ask you if you believe in God.

ROALD. I *don't*.

LICCY. But people don't ask off the bat – it's *personal*.

ROALD. Is it? I thought it was highly pertinent.

LICCY. I'm sure Mrs Stone's professionalism is unquestionable.

ROALD. Of course. What makes you think it isn't? Tut, Liccy. So is that a no or a yes?

Beat.

JESSIE. Well, I. Yes. I'm Jewish, yes.

ROALD. You don't sound sure. Want to make a phone call?

JESSIE. No. I'm certain.

ROALD. There you are. Wasn't so hard, was it? And do you practise? All the waving around the scrolls and the funny tassels and the fasting and whatnot.

JESSIE. We celebrate the big festivals.

ROALD. Ah, the fun stuff. I know that trick. I tried to go once. Church. Seriously, you know. Every day. After my Olivia died. Worked for a bit. But the scales soon fell from my eyes.

JESSIE. Well it's an important part of our lives. But it's not for everyone.

ROALD. Being Jewish?

JESSIE. No. Ha. No, religion. Ritual.

ROALD. Heaven is certainly not for everyone. Including dogs. I have it on absolute authority. Archbishop of Canterbury.

LICCY. Really?

ROALD. Would be a deeply strange lie to tell, Lis. I'm sure I told you, I went to see him, asked about our dog who'd just popped off. He said no. No animals in heaven. Like some celestial park warden. No souls, you see. So I told him to stuff it. No dogs, no Dahl.

Beat.

TOM (*to* ROALD). So how do you want to kick this off?

ROALD. Well I just wanted to get a sense of who's who. Mrs Stone, forgive my directness.

JESSIE. No no, I understand.

ROALD. I am a direct sort.

JESSIE. Yes.

ROALD. And in the spirit of directness, how do you feel about Israel? Presume you're a fan.

LICCY. I'm not sure that's…

ROALD. Well I daresay it is. I dare say it's *everything*.

JESSIE. Uh –

ROALD. I'd like to know whom I'm talking to. Mrs Stone?

JESSIE. Well. I'm Jewish. I'm American. So.

ROALD. Fan.

JESSIE. Well, that's not what I – it's not a given.

ROALD. But likely.

JESSIE. Not everyone has the same –

ROALD. Of course, yes, there's those tiny-weeny progressives – the New Israel Fund, I know about them – (*To* JESSIE.) but they're really a minor player, no? Seen as crazies?

JESSIE. Are they?

ROALD. Tiny crazy gang of peace-loving bleeding-heart hippies. Hardly the main swim.

JESSIE. Is that right?

ROALD. I'm asking you.

JESSIE. You seem to have a strong grasp of it all.

Beat.

ROALD. Is that you then? Crazy peace-loving American hippy?

JESSIE (*confused*). I'm. I think we're – what are you asking, exactly?

ROALD. Just where you fundamentally stand. So I'm clear.

Beat.

JESSIE. I believe Israel has the right to exist.

ROALD. Ah. Unconditionally?

JESSIE. Well it's a *country.* Sovereign. Recognised by international law. Created by the United Nations. What conditions do you have in mind?

Beat. They could jump off here. But is this the moment?

ROALD (*winks*). So you're not a peace-loving hippy?

JESSIE. I'm definitely peace-loving!

ROALD. Phew!

JESSIE. Not a hippy so much – smoked a little pot in college but –

ROALD (*mock-dramatic*). Criminal in our midst! Call the constable! Citizens' arrest! (*Confidentially.*) I smoked pot once too. Oof. No hippy, I. Something in common there, at least.

Beat.

TOM. Well, good –

JESSIE. I'm also able to see Israel's mistakes and flaws.

ROALD. Ha. Sounds like how I talk about Colin, Liccy.

LICCY. Does it?

ROALD. I have an old friend. Colin. Always skint, always – well that's another story. But – it's familiar. I can see all his foibles, as it were. As you can with Israel. But I'm still very fond of him. As you still seem to be with Israel. Colin is my Israel, I suppose. Always punching people and blaming the barman.

TOM. Mrs Stone will give you valuable, impartial advice –

ROALD. Oh will she?

TOM. – about the possible impact of this situation on your American book sales.

ROALD. Right.

TOM. As will I for the British market. That's why we're here.

LICCY. That's why they're here, Roald.

TOM. That's why Roger sent her. You can trust in our professional objectivity, Roald.

ROALD. But that's what I don't know, Tom. That's why I'm asking. Can I not ask?

Uncomfortable pause.

JESSIE. Shall I – ?

TOM. Yes.

ROALD. Shall she, what?

TOM. Start?

ROALD. I thought we very much had.

Beat.

JESSIE. Mr Dahl, the pressure on our end is that *The New York Times* called FSG. Yesterday. To know if you stand by your comments.

ROALD. Why would I have made them? Yes! Of course! What did you say?

JESSIE. That we would talk to you first.

ROALD. Why? What on earth did you think I'd – ? 'Oops, my mistake, take it all back'? You needn't have flown halfway round the world to ask me that. Say yes. Yes, I stand by my comments. Firmly.

Beat.

JESSIE. We believe that they'll run a damaging article and your new book will suffer.

ROALD. Nonsense.

LICCY. Don't just say nonsense.

ROALD. *Fantastic* nonsense, then. Who buys my books? Children. They don't read the fucking *Spectator* or *The New*

York bloody *Times*. I mean one or two might – heaven knows some children are really quite odd –

TOM. I think the storm here in the UK –

ROALD. Storm? It's really –

TOM. Fine – hoo-ha –

LICCY. There's a lot of / *reaction.*

ROALD (*to* LICCY). You bundling on now?

TOM. – plus a possible New York pile-on –

ROALD (*mocking*). – 'the most despicable something ever written in English ever'! Jumped-up fanny. Did you see that, Mrs Stone? Unbelievable, no?

Beat.

Silence from my publisher. Or are you here to panic me? Panic an old man.

Beat. He looks at JESSIE.

Because I'm sure you'd love it if I issued an apology. Given your feelings about Colin.

Beat.

JESSIE. I just want the best for your book.

ROALD. So you *do*!

TOM. She's giving you the bare facts, not –

ROALD (*sardonic*). No, no, of course –

TOM. She wants you to have the context.

JESSIE, *beginning to boil, struggles not to speak her mind.*

JESSIE (*pushing forward*). Mr Straus wants to convey very clearly that if *The New York Times* attacks you, we might also lose the ALA.

TOM (*to* LICCY). The librarians.

LICCY. Yes yes we know them well.

ROALD. God. Satan's Spinster Army. Gluttons for a wholesome message.

TOM. Libraries in every town, every high school.

ROALD. Alright, Tom, it's not a disaster movie. (*Mock-American movie accent.*) 'Every town, every high school.' Dearie me.

TOM. It's a brilliant fucking book, Roald.

ROALD. How good? Because I need a bit of balance here. The cup of cheer is fast draining.

TOM. I love it. All our key readers do. And sales-wise, we're sure it'll at least match *BFG*.

ROALD. At least?

TOM. At *least*. But I want more than that. It should outsell *BFG*. That's where you are now. Deservedly so.

Beat. ROALD *considers this, likes it, but needs some more love.*

ROALD. Mrs Stone? Little Archie get a sneak preview? (*From her reaction.*) Aha! Snuck it out the office for him, you scamp! And...?

JESSIE. He enjoyed it very much. Found it scary for sure –

ROALD. At fifteen?

LICCY. Why not?

JESSIE. Well those witches are – very scary.

LICCY. Wait till you see Quentin's new cover!

JESSIE. And Roger's hugely excited.

ROALD. About the book or the sales?

JESSIE. Both. Absolutely. We all are.

TOM. But we have to be strategic. Even without the *Times* egging them on, we can't guarantee the librarians will love a coven of diabolical, child-pulping witches.

ROALD. Won't they rejoice that their story is *finally* being told?

LICCY. Nor the boy who *stays* as a mouse and *dies* with his grandmother.

ROALD (*playfully defensive*). Alright, Liccy.

TOM. We have to manage this. Like it or not.

ROALD. She hates the ending.

TOM. And we can.

LICCY. I do not. It's just sad. Profoundly sad.

TOM. We ought to respond.

ROALD. No.

TOM. Somehow.

ROALD. No and no.

TOM. All publicity's good – *even* attacks – as long as the book's in fucking stock. You had this with *Charlie*. Why not now?

ROALD. Different.

TOM. How?

ROALD. The NAACP chaps were right. You can't have pygmy Oompa Loompas. And that was in the book. This situation, unrelated.

JESSIE. Is it?

ROALD. Yes. The present hoo-ha is about some off-piste book review I wrote.

JESSIE shifts uncomfortably.

Yes?

JESSIE. Yeah. Yes. Yeah.

ROALD. Yes. Yeah. Jet-lag speaking?

JESSIE. Well… there are *things*. In the book itself. That might be construed as…

ROALD. What?

TOM (*sensing danger*). We don't need to worry about construed.

ROALD. She clearly does.

TOM. Let's not pick at details.

ROALD (*to* JESSIE). What?

Beat. She looks at ROALD. *At* TOM, *who's glaring as subtly as he can.*

JESSIE. Do you not see that, in a certain context, in the context of your review, people might interpret *The Witches* perhaps… as… analogous?

ROALD. To the oppression of the Palestinian people?

JESSIE. To certain stereotypes.

ROALD. What stereotypes?

TOM. This is really *detail* –

JESSIE. Well, Mr Dahl, it's a book about a secret society –

ROALD. Yes?

JESSIE. – of powerful, child-snatching, money-printing devils, posing as humans.

ROALD. Thank you for describing my book *The Witches* by me, Roald Dahl.

JESSIE. And –

TOM (*steers a hard right*). But if we get mauled in the States –

ROALD. Stop catastrophising, Tom! 'Mauled.' They're not bears.

TOM. – we can't risk the librarians taking it off the shelves –

ROALD. There's still bookshops, it'll be in bookshops. (*To* JESSIE.) She knows. Plenty of bookshops to sell it in.

Beat. JESSIE *shifts again in her seat.* ROALD *stares at her.*

What stereotypes?

JESSIE. Nothing. I was –

ROALD. 'Nothing' is already worse than the answer you aren't giving.

Beat.

JESSIE. Of Jews. Jews have been stereotyped as demons. And devils. Who stalk the land. And print money. And kill children. For pleasure and gain.

ROALD. They have?

JESSIE. Yes. For centuries.

ROALD. Fucking hell. Now I've written an allegory.

LICCY. This really is a bit much.

TOM. She's giving you a *context* –

LICCY. It's *ridiculous*.

ROALD. Now I've written a secret coded hate tract. Have you ever? It's about my grandmother! About my childhood! It's about finding love at the point of death! It's not about the bloody Jews! Talk about seeing it where it isn't!

TOM. She thinks others *might* see that.

ROALD. Who?

Beat. JESSIE, *under the glare of* ROALD*'s scrutiny, is trying to keep focused under fire.*

JESSIE. There's a man. Mr Taft.

ROALD. Is he outside with a cocked Glock?

LICCY. Don't, Roald.

ROALD. Should I get under the table?

LICCY. Not funny. *Not* funny.

JESSIE. He runs a local bookstore in a beautiful little town Upstate.

ROALD (*mock-horror*). A *whole* bookshop?

JESSIE. He stocks everything we publish and has a strong customer base. He wrote to us last week to say he'd no longer be taking your books. Not *The Witches*, not the back catalogue.

ROALD. Jewish, I assume?

JESSIE. Yes. And he went through the Holocaust.

LICCY. Ah.

JESSIE. The camps. And very supportive of Israel.

ROALD. Needless to say.

LICCY (*trying to be reasonable, empathetic*). Well they are, aren't they? Makes sense, of course. After all they suffered.

ROALD. Except Tom, of course. The only one who got out of Hitler's Germany entirely unflustered.

TOM. I was a little boy.

ROALD. An unflustered little Maschler. Even the Reich couldn't knock him off-stride.

Beat.

JESSIE. He was very upset by your comments.

ROALD. So? We lose a bookshop! Is this really worth discussing?!

Beat.

JESSIE. The thing is, Mr Dahl – and it's the only reason I raise it – he's part of a network of shops. Quite a big one. He represents more.

ROALD. How many more?

JESSIE. Hundreds by association.

TOM. Bloody hell.

JESSIE. It's not that it will happen. It's just that it might. It might.

ROALD. Might. Might might might might might might.

Pause. ROALD *is momentarily stilled by this accumulation of evidence.*

TOM. We need to say something.

JESSIE nods in agreement. ROALD stops to think, stews, cornered, hating this. Looks at LICCY. *She's on* TOM*'s side.*

ROALD. Is this the tack now, Tom? Can't write anything about Israel because of the Holocaust? Is that what you're saying, Mrs Stone?

Pause. Eventually:

TOM. Do you know Annabel Levene at the *Mail on Sunday*?

ROALD. No. Vaguely. Perhaps.

TOM. Features writer, Jewish, which helps us, but not *jewishjewish* which wouldn't, / of course –

JESSIE. I'm sorry?

TOM. What?

JESSIE. What does that mean? Not jewishjewish?

TOM. Not overly, you know, aggressively, Jewish.

JESSIE. Aggressively?

TOM. Yes.

JESSIE (*under her breath in disbelief*). Wow.

TOM. I'm sorry?

JESSIE. Nothing. I mean I got that she's Jewish. But *twice*?

TOM (*sharp*). A little calm now, Mrs Stone.

ROALD. Now now, children.

TOM. Think we can all do with a little calm.

Beat.

She does those big weekend profiles, just did Bob Hope and before that uh Princess Leia…

LICCY. Carrie Fisher.

TOM. Yes.

LICCY (*to* ROALD). Debbie Reynolds' daughter.

ROALD. I *know* who Carrie Fisher is, Liccy.

TOM. Anyway, we do a spread with her –

ROALD. Christ, Lis, I'm not ninety. Don't need people explained by their parentage.

TOM. – celebrate the new-look house, *The Witches* –

ROALD. That great antisemitic polemic!

ACT ONE   45

TOM. – and she gets *one* question about this. One. And I'll tell them nothing accusatory or loaded, no follow-ups either. Just an opportunity for Roald to say something in response, something conciliatory –

ROALD. I don't want to be conciliatory.

TOM. – fine, self-aware –

ROALD. I'm wildly self-aware –

TOM. – to acknowledge that this is a divisive issue, complexity on both sides, you can talk about your passionate support for Palestine –

ROALD (*ironic*). Oh may I?

TOM. – for children of all backgrounds, mention your wider charity work, give them context, and that, if there is offence caused, you're sorry for it. Something like that. And FSG can use it pre-emptively against any further backlash in the States, even if you *don't* actually concede any ground. I think it will go a long way to killing it dead.

   JESSIE *is deeply unsettled.*

ROALD. Your colleague's gone all pasty-faced.

JESSIE. Have I?

TOM. Has she?

ROALD. All twitchy and pasty.

LICCY. Roald.

ROALD. But she has.

TOM. Mrs Stone?

JESSIE. Well, uh –

TOM. Is there – ?

JESSIE. No, it's –

TOM (*to* JESSIE, *irritated*). You'll have, in effect, a statement from Roald –

ROALD. Twitch, twitch.

TOM. – which FSG can quote – for the *Times*, for anyone.

JESSIE. It won't be –

ROALD. Ah…

TOM. *What*, Mrs Stone?

Beat.

JESSIE. With all due respect, why go to all this trouble if the message won't actually *persuade* the people we're concerned about?

ROALD. You here to protect me or them?

TOM. It's something to work with. Something which doesn't compromise our author.

Beat. JESSIE*'s anger is now cutting through her professional mask.*

JESSIE. You say 'work with', but 'sorry if I've caused offence' doesn't account for what… what was said in the first place.

TOM. Our – your – only job here is to smooth a path for sales.

JESSIE. But it won't if the statement is so *limited*.

TOM. You can't know that.

JESSIE. I do.

TOM (*sarcastic*). 'Won't.'

JESSIE. I know, Mr Maschler.

TOM. How?

JESSIE. Because I talk to our networks.

TOM. But how can you possibly know?!

JESSIE. We *talk* to them –

TOM. And at these coffee mornings, what do –

ROALD (*suddenly*). *Ding-a-ling-a-ling!*

TOM. Yes?

ROALD. During this charming song of unity, I made a thrilling decision. And it's a big fat pig of a no.

TOM. To her question?

ROALD. To her. To this tacit genuflex.

TOM. It loses us nothing. Only gains.

ROALD. It's a Trojan horse and I despise Trojan horses.

LICCY. It's better than silence, surely?

ROALD (*to* LICCY). Et tu?

TOM. You're wrong, Roald, / it's a really elegant solution.

ROALD. DON'T FUCKING TELL ME I'M WRONG, TOM! I'm not apologising to those people!

TOM. It's not an apology.

ROALD. It's a *FUCKING* apology! What else could it possibly be?

TOM. It's a concession to the validity of another point of view! That's all we need you to say.

ROALD. There *is* no validity!! There is no fucking validity!! Why do I – ? And whatever I say, it won't be enough. (*Of* JESSIE.) Ask *her*! She knows them. She *is* them. NOTHING will be enough! So why give them anything at all?!

A long silence. ROALD *twinges in pain, twitches sulkily, then stands.*

I must get back to work.

LICCY. There's pudding.

ROALD. I'll take it in the shed. Where are my matches?

LICCY. On the shelf. I'll get them.

ROALD (*to* JESSIE). And have a safe journey home.

As he labours towards the garden:

Oh and please leave the pencils here.

He pulls out a hanky then turns, looks back at JESSIE.

And one other thing. Loose end. Been niggling.

JESSIE. Yes.

ROALD. Did you say you read to him?

JESSIE. I'm sorry?

ROALD. Your boy. Did you say you read to him? At fifteen.

LICCY. Why?

ROALD. Struck me as odd.

LICCY. *I* read to my youngest for ages –

ROALD. Not at fifteen. Ten, eleven *perhaps*, but…

Beat. JESSIE *uncomfortable under* ROALD*'s scrutiny.*

Was it acquired?

Beat. They look at each other.

JESSIE. No.

ROALD. Hm. One develops an instinct. My eldest acquired his. Awful term, but… Taxi careered into his pram. Acquired or not, no one else understands. Like stepping into a new world, over a line you didn't know existed.

JESSIE. Yes.

ROALD. You have to keep at them. Don't let them slide. Keep at them. Reading! Reading is a great medicine! Builds the brain back up.

Beat.

JESSIE (*surprised*). Thank you.

ROALD. Well. Goodbye. Safe journey home.

ROALD *puts the hanky over his mouth and shuffles out into the garden. Silence.*

TOM. I should go too. Not much more I can do.

He gets up.

LICCY. Tom, stay.

TOM. He won't budge.

ACT ONE   49

LICCY. *Sit.*

He sits.

I'll talk to him, but if he listens to me, you two are next up. You'll have to say something.

TOM. *She'll* have to say something.

JESSIE (*stunned*). Why?

TOM. 'Why?'

LICCY. Certainly a change of tack is needed.

JESSIE. I'm sorry, Mrs Crosland, but *he* –

LICCY. As maybe, but he's also your author. No?

JESSIE stops – there's too much to unpack here.

I see that this is complicated but let me be frank – Roald has spent years, long before I knew him, supporting destitute people, children especially, around the world. Lebanon broke his heart. Truly. Mine too. So, whatever you think about what he wrote, it comes from a place of passion, and now really isn't the moment to let your own beliefs –

JESSIE. They're not my –

LICCY. Don't interrupt. To let your own beliefs influence events. Nor can we force his hand.

JESSIE. But I didn't – I didn't force anything –

LICCY. You told your star author his new novel is a racist analogy!

JESSIE. I didn't – I'm sorry, but –

LICCY. You let him glimpse your critical notes.

JESSIE. They fell out – !

LICCY. You grumped and groaned at his every other comment!

JESSIE (*utter disbelief*). Oh my god, I – (*Stops herself.*) With the greatest respect, Mrs Crosland, for whatever reason, Mr Dahl singled me out the moment I stepped in this room. I was trying to be professional –

LICCY. By being an hour late?

JESSIE. – but – sure, okay, not an hour –

LICCY. As good as.

JESSIE. It wasn't, but –

LICCY. – forty-eight minutes, / so sorry –

JESSIE. – but what am I supposed to do, to say, when he's so direct? Nothing?

TOM. Yes!

JESSIE. What, be silent? Just sit there mute –

TOM. Deflect, deflect!

JESSIE. It's crazy.

TOM. It's your job.

LICCY. Manage the author.

JESSIE. And, anyway, it was Mr Maschler's proposal he rejected.

LICCY. Because he felt hemmed in.

JESSIE. Because he *is*, Ms Crosland. By… the reaction. Not by me. By newspapers, by people. Yes, I have differences of opinion, but I was –

LICCY. It would help if you just recognised you've gone too far. I know that some of what was said was difficult to take. These things sit at the core of who we are. But he's on edge, he's in pain – try to take him with a pinch of salt. You understand?

JESSIE. Yes.

LICCY. I for one – and Roald I'm sure – would appreciate it. Roger too.

   JESSIE *nods, muted*.

   Tom, can you see where he is?

   TOM *peers out*.

TOM. He's talking to your Big Friendly Gardener.

LICCY. Well, I'll leave you to work out the details. (*Calls offstage.*) Hallie! (*As she goes out.*) Fumes gone? Can't smell it now...

TOM *rocks back, irate, looks at this watch. They sit in silence a moment, processing.*

TOM. When the managing director of a major publishing house leaves you a message ahead of a big tricky meeting, the thing you do is – call me bloody back.

JESSIE. I apologise, Mr Maschler. It's our first vacation as a family in three years. I really thought you were just saying hello.

TOM. 'Hello'? I'm Roger's British counterpart, not your buddy. I needed to brief you! Which, as you can see, works much more effectively *before* the meeting.

JESSIE. I'm sorry.

JESSIE *looks away.*

TOM. The witches are an analogy for the Jews! What's fucking wrong with you?

JESSIE (*provoked*). No, that's – he wrote a book review calling for the destruction of the State of Israel. A *book review* calling the Jews of the world – *all* Jews – immoral cowards if they don't disavow Israel. Comparing Israel to Nazi Germany.

TOM. And?

JESSIE. People might be forgiven for seeing a bit of *coded* antisemitism after reading reams of the *un*coded sort.

TOM. People like you?

JESSIE (*standing fast*). People.

TOM. He doesn't want those people *in his living room*.

JESSIE. I don't even know if he understands what he's saying.

TOM. Irrelevant.

JESSIE. If he did maybe he'd be more open to the idea.

TOM. We are not about to re-educate him! Fuck's sake, Mrs Stone! No, no, no. The whole point of Roger sending you here – (*Low, remembering* HALLIE *next door.*) the whole *point* of his *pretending* to Roald you flew in from New York overnight – was to make a show, make him feel flattered and fawned over. To protect him. From others, from himself. Because when he doesn't feel those things – when he senses neglect or, I don't know, judgement and condemnation – he leaves!

Pause.

I wanted to put you bang in the picture. Apprise you of the difficulties. Because, in case you hadn't noticed, he's a human fucking boobytrap! And now, guess what, surprise surprise, boom!

TOM, *agitated, glances out into the garden.*

They're talking. That's something.

He looks at his watch.

Tut.

He looks out to the garden again.

(*Softens slightly.*) Look, I'm sorry your big family holiday's been interrupted. I can only imagine how tricky it is – especially with your boy – but when – *if* – he comes back in, just say sorry. If we both do it, we'll look like a dance troupe, and if it's just me, it won't settle him. Okay?

Long pause. JESSIE *chews on this.* TOM *watches her, then looks outside, then back to her.*

(*Snapping.*) What are you *thinking* about now? Stop fucking thinking. You really want to be traipsing round Washington Square next week clutching your CV? Have your moment of conscience here and you'll forever be the person who lost FSG Roald Dahl. The woman who couldn't keep her mouth shut. And who wants to hire one of those?

Beat.

JESSIE. What if he comes back and I apologise and, after all that, he refuses to comment at all?

TOM. He'll say something.

JESSIE. Because he seems pretty – *entrenched*.

TOM. I'm a skilful unentrencher.

JESSIE. And if you can't?

TOM. What do you want us to do?

JESSIE. Myriad options.

TOM. Chastise him publicly? Drop him? Are you fucking / kidding me?

JESSIE. Is Israel really the Fourth Reich? You survived the third.

TOM (*mock-drama*). 'Survived'!

JESSIE. What?

TOM. I was a boy. I got on a fucking train.

JESSIE. Fine. You escaped certain death by getting on a train. Are you really happy to be silent about that?

TOM. Yes! Yes, I am! Because books are how we grow up. How we first navigate the world, learn to live, become vaguely functioning adults. And this man, he deserves criticism for what he's said, sure, but, in his books, he… picks a glorious, playful path through the chaos of childhood. It's the rarest of gifts. To show its cruelty but take you out the other side. And the more kids feel guided by his books, the more boldly they'll read as adults, and rise above the narrow crap their parents told them to sit with braver minds in richer worlds. So I won't *drop* him. Not for this. And if someone thinks I tacitly approve of his childish views on Israel because I didn't speak out against them, I'll take it.

TOM *goes to the builders' sheets.*

JESSIE. And if you speak out, you might sell fewer books.

TOM. Yeah that too. Ah! Here they come. Well done, Lis, you clever thing.

He smiles, waves to them.

(*To* JESSIE.) You're lucky his back's fucked. Gives you an extra five seconds to plan your speech of contrition.

He lifts one of the builders' sheets.

And yawn more. You've got jet-lag remember. If he sniffs
Roger's ruse, we'll be bird food. Okay? (*Calls to* ROALD.)
Come on, slowcoach.

ROALD *and* LICCY *enter. He's hot, mopping his brow and holding a sprig of leaves.*

ROALD. There's a lovely leafy tunnel which leads to my hut.
Wally planted it about twelve years ago. And this time of
year it's absolutely on fire, pong-wise. Amazing. Whiff?

He gives it to JESSIE *to smell, she does.*

JESSIE. Wonderful. Yes, wow.

She passes it to TOM, *who takes it reluctantly.*

ROALD. Tom knows it well.

TOM. Still, smashing. We have eucalyptus. Floods the air.

ROALD. This trumps eucalyptus.

TOM *smells it again.*

TOM. Dead heat.

ROALD. No contest.

TOM (*concedes*). Very nice.

He hands it back to ROALD.

ROALD (*smiles*). You've spoken?

TOM. Yes.

ROALD. And?

JESSIE. Mr Dahl, I just wanted you to know that I'm sorry for
suggesting you do more than is comfortable. This is an
incredibly difficult situation for you, Mrs Crosland, a lot of
stress and worry, and it was selfish and unhelpful of me to
say what I did.

Beat.

ROALD. Yes. Yes. So why the fuck did you?

LICCY. Roald –

JESSIE. Sorry?

LICCY. – we just discussed this.

ROALD (*to* JESSIE). Say it!

JESSIE. I don't, I –

ROALD (*mocking*). You don't, you – ?

JESSIE. I –

LICCY. Please.

ROALD. Yes?

JESSIE. My own thoughts on this are irrelevant, Mr Dahl. I just want to help you get the book out in the States with minimal –

ROALD. Yes yes… But your thoughts pulse in another direction, no?

LICCY. She's just apologised…

JESSIE. My personal position is totally –

ROALD. In what precise way is my review so offensive?

JESSIE *glances at* TOM.

(*To* JESSIE.) Don't look at him. Look at me.

JESSIE. I don't…

ROALD. Just for japes.

JESSIE. I was just… my thoughts were related to work. That booksellers felt they couldn't – stock you – if they felt you… if you didn't… so I was trying to reflect their concerns back to you.

ROALD. I see. Well, might you deliver a message to *them* – Mr Taft, is it?

JESSIE. Of course.

ROALD. Perhaps write it down, avoid inaccuracies.

JESSIE *grabs a pen and notebook from her bag*.

Please tell him that it is now upon *his* head, that the kinder – children is 'kinder', Tom, in Yiddish?

TOM. Yes.

ROALD. – yes, that the kinder of his shtetl in upstate Noo Yoik will have to make do – no, *survive* on a strictly kosher diet of Helen Oxenberry and Sue Townsend.

JESSIE. Yes.

ROALD. Poor little buggers. He will starve them of Dahl. And they will revolt. And then we'll see how he feeds his tiny Tafts.

LICCY. Enough.

ROALD. He won't stock me and I'm happy not to be stocked. Now, let's finish lunch, shall we? Alright, Tom?

TOM. Yes.

LICCY (*calls*). Hallie?

ROALD. Sure?

ROALD *looks at* JESSIE – *a test – then back at* TOM.

TOM. Yes, why do you ask? Pudding, terrific.

ROALD. Good! No objections from Tom. I spied something excellent in the fridge.

LICCY (*calls*). Hallie!

HALLIE (*off*). Yes?

LICCY (*calls*). Pudding please.

ROALD. The prospect of which has kept me perky throughout this sapping affair.

ROALD *sparks up a cigarette.* HALLIE, *entering with dessert, notices the charged atmosphere.*

Hallie, what sweet delights have we in store?

HALLIE. Great, well, nothing major –

ROALD. She always says that.

HALLIE. – I've made two sorbets from garden fruit – a plum and a pear –

ROALD. Lovely.

HALLIE. – and added some mint as a little kicker. And there's some berries. And a sprinkle of Krokaan.

ACT ONE   57

ROALD. Oof. (*To* HALLIE, *pronunciation*.) Krok*aa*n.

HALLIE. Krok*aa*n.

LICCY (*to* TOM, JESSIE). Norwegian specialty. Come come sit.

ROALD. Caramel crunch. Oof. Hallie's is nearly as good as my grandmother's.

HALLIE. Nearly?

ROALD (*teasing*). By a smidgeon.

   HALLIE *starts to serve*.

   Bit more, bit more.

HALLIE. Of this?

ROALD. No, the plum.

   HALLIE *hands* ROALD *his plate*.

LICCY. Garden mint too.

ROALD. No no. Krokaan.

LICCY (*of dessert*). Mrs Stone?

ROALD (*to* HALLIE). More more. Yum yum. Plum plum.

JESSIE (*barely containing her fury*). What do you think they're so angry about, Mr Dahl?

TOM (*quiet, sharp, to* JESSIE). No.

LICCY (*to* JESSIE). Try the sorbet *with* the crunch?

JESSIE (*to* ROALD). These Jews. What do you think it is exactly?

TOM (*to* JESSIE) No. No. No.

HALLIE (*of dessert*) Mr Maschler?

JESSIE (*to* ROALD). Pure irrational meanness?

LICCY (*to* JESSIE, *of her dessert*). Why not get that down you?

ROALD (*to* JESSIE). Taft's your friend, ask him.

LICCY. We all deserve a little breather, don't you think?

JESSIE stands in anger.

JESSIE. Mr Taft is angry that you – that your review –

TOM. How are the girls, Roald?

JESSIE. – that it's driven –

TOM. Wasn't it Sophie's birthday last week?

LICCY. September.

TOM. Oh. This September?

LICCY. Every September.

JESSIE. That it's driven by some incendiary ideas.

ROALD. *Good!* Incendiary's good. We need a bit of fire. (*To* TOM, *of proof.*) Now – this is one – did Quent definitely redo this?

TOM. Let me see.

ROALD. It looks suspiciously familiar.

JESSIE pulls Roald's review from her bag and starts to read it aloud.

JESSIE. 'In June 1941 I happened to be in of all places Palestine, flying with the RAF against the Vichy French and the Nazis. Hitler happened to be in Germany and the gas chambers were being built and the mass slaughter of the Jews was beginning. Our hearts bled for the Jewish men, women and children, and we hated the Germans.'

TOM. What the fuck are you doing?

JESSIE. 'Exactly forty-one years later' –

TOM. He knows what he wrote!

JESSIE. '…in June 1982 the Israeli forces were streaming northwards out of what used to be Palestine into Lebanon and the mass slaughter of the inhabitants began. Our hearts bled for the Lebanese and Palestinian men, women and children and we all started hating the Israelis. Never before in the history of man has a race of people switched so rapidly from being much pitied victims to barbarous murderers. Never

ACT ONE 59

before has a race of people generated so much sympathy around the world and then, in the space of a lifetime, succeeded in turning that sympathy into hatred and revulsion.'

TOM. Finished?

JESSIE (*reads on*). 'It is as though a group of much loved nuns in charge of an orphanage had suddenly turned round and started murdering all the children.'

Beat.

TOM. Rain stops fucking play.

ROALD. She's terrific, she should do the cassette recordings.

JESSIE. It's *why* people are upset. / Not because –

ROALD. What's more upsetting besides those fuckers bombing civilians and children?

JESSIE. Not because –

ROALD. Besides how decency and honour must out.

JESSIE. Not because you don't have the right to criticise Israel.

ROALD. Thank you, kindly.

JESSIE. But because all the politics is mixed in with a stiff measure of something else.

TOM. Stop! Now! Stop, Stone. Stop. Force fucking majeure! Sorry, Roald. Sorry. No. We don't need this. We, I, came here to advise you, put you in the picture –

ROALD. – force an apology –

TOM. – then *leave* – what? *No*. Not 'force' –

JESSIE. You've written a rave review of a scathing book about Israel –

ROALD. About Beirut, about Beiruti *anguish*, but if you must make everything about Israel –

JESSIE. – okay, about Beirut then, about the Israeli siege of Beirut, so sorry – in which the Israelis – all Israelis, all Jews in fact – are drawn as 'barbarous murderers'. Do you see what I'm saying?

ROALD. They fired guided missiles into seven of the ten hospitals in Beirut, packed with children, into a mental hospital, so what are you saying?

JESSIE. That an entire race of people is being blamed for the actions of the Israeli army.

Pause.

What happened in Beirut, Mr Dahl, pains many Jews. *Many.*

ROALD. Well that's very nice.

JESSIE. The loss of civilian life is unbearable, hard to reconcile, even for many Jews, with –

ROALD. What? The great Israeli project?

LICCY. Let her *speak* –

JESSIE. With what Israel stands for. What it was created to be –

ROALD. An apartheid fun palace?

JESSIE. – no! no! A liberal, progressive / democracy –

ROALD. Well if it irks Jews so, they should march, speak out –

JESSIE. But they *do*! – (*Corrects.*) Four hundred thousand Israelis protested the siege in Tel Aviv, protested Sharon, and the Supreme Court forced him out of the army – but – here – in your review, you just lump every Jew in together. All Israelis – even though many resist – and all Jews – as if we're all in cahoots. The Jews. The Jewish race. Jews. A single organism. But Mr Maschler isn't Israeli. So is he responsible for bombing hospitals? Is he a beast?

ROALD. Bestial.

JESSIE. Bestial.

ROALD. Are you bestial, Tom?

TOM. On grass, absolutely.

JESSIE. Am *I*?

ROALD. Now that *is* a question.

JESSIE (*reads*). '*God Cried* is a terrific book,' you say. 'Every Jew in the world should read it. So should everyone who has any conscience at all. Now is the time for the Jews of the world to become anti-Israeli. But do they have the conscience? And do they I wonder, have the guts? Or must Israel, like Germany' – you mean Nazi Germany – 'be brought to its knees before she learns how to behave in the world?' Should Mr Maschler atone? Should I?

ROALD. No, turns out that's my treat for today.

JESSIE. And if we don't, what are we? Innate cowards? All of us, to a man?

ROALD. I think you might be overthinking this.

JESSIE. Overthinking *what*, *Mr Dahl*? You just made me write down an *antisemitic* 'letter' to a Jewish client –

ROALD. I was trying –

JESSIE. – and now you tell me I'm seeing what isn't there?!

ROALD. I was trying to jolt you out of your deluded reverence.

JESSIE. For who?

ROALD. People like Mr Taft can't control the entire conversation simply because of what they suffered.

JESSIE. He's not controlling *anything*!

ROALD. He demands *I* apologise!

JESSIE. He's a sweet man who owns a nice bookshop in the Hudson Valley, not a controlling overlord! He's just outraged you wrote an article craving the destruction of the State of Israel! The only thing his suffering's good for is a pretty good read on racial hatred.

ROALD. And that's what this is?

Beat.

JESSIE. You don't believe Israel should exist, do you?

ROALD. Good god.

TOM. Will you stop now?

ROALD. Oh that'll do it, Tom.

JESSIE. Because if you did, you might have mentioned, once, somewhere, anywhere, that Israel invaded Lebanon in self-defence.

ROALD. Will someone please turn her off? I need a fucking pee.

JESSIE. The PLO fired hundreds and hundreds of rockets from Southern Lebanon into Israel. At schools, at children.

ROALD. Find the bloody button.

JESSIE. For days and days. Two summers in a row.

ROALD. Is there, is there a plug?

JESSIE. Scrambling into shelters. But in your review, the Israelis just show up in Beirut like fiends of hell to destroy a cowering city.

ROALD. They disregarded the Beirutis' humanity, so why must I imbue them with any?

JESSIE. What would your government do if militants *constitutionally* committed to wiping Britain off the map started firing rockets into Kent from the French coast? For ten days? Serve tea and scones?

ROALD. They wouldn't lay waste a city!

JESSIE. Dresden, Nagasaki?

ROALD. How dare you compare them?!

JESSIE. Why, because you spent the war doing loop-de-loops in your fighter plane, like David Niven? Because the British couldn't be anything other than the saviours of humanity, whilst those fucking Jews can only be monsters! And because if it's self-defence it would suggest – *god forbid!* – they have a rightful country to defend.

They stare at each other.

You saved the Jews in Europe only to find the Jews weren't worth saving. And now you want their devil-state brought to its knees?

ROALD. And what do you want?

JESSIE. I'm asking you to apologise!

ROALD. To who?

JESSIE. To them!

ROALD. To *you*! To *you*, Stein!

JESSIE. Just apologise! You understand the power of language more than anyone! How it can twist things out of shape. And how it can make things whole again. And this kind of language, when the world comes for us again, when people like you won't protect us any more – well it sends me and my son somewhere Mr Taft knows only too well. So, yes, yes, you do. Owe me an apology. *Yes*, yes. Yes, sir. Yes, you do.

End Act One.

ACT TWO

Minutes later. HALLIE *collects the dirty dessert plates, and* LICCY *sets clean ones. Muted sounds of* TOM *on the phone upstairs. A toilet flushes in the house.* HALLIE *goes into the kitchen.* ROALD *comes in.*

ROALD. Oof.

LICCY. Okay.

ROALD. Narrow escape.

LICCY. Thank god.

ROALD. Battle adrenaline meant I held it in, but…

LICCY. That's wonderful.

> LICCY *continues to neaten the table.*

ROALD. But then –

LICCY. Would you like a cigarette?

ROALD. Who's Spootlicker yakking with?

LICCY. Trying to get hold of his tennis chum.

ROALD. Cancelling, I assume. The dragon? Still – [*outside*]?

LICCY. Yes.

> HALLIE *comes in with the sorbet tubs.*

HALLIE. Sorbet, take two?

ROALD (*greedily*). Mmmmm.

HALLIE. Plum or pear?

ROALD. And, and.

> HALLIE *opens the lid, starts to serve a greedy-eyed* ROALD. TOM *comes back in from the house, frustrated.*

LICCY. Get him?

TOM. No. His wife. He'd already gone.

LICCY. Ah, well.

ROALD. Poor little Ian McEwan, alone on the baseline, cursing Tommy Maschler.

HALLIE (*of sorbet*). Miss Crosland?

ROALD. 'That dastardly Spootlicker!'

LICCY. No no.

ROALD. Boo.

HALLIE. Mr Maschler?

TOM. No.

ROALD. To eat sorbet alone is a terrible thing.

Beat.

What do you think, darling girl?

HALLIE. Of what?

ROALD. All this?

HALLIE. Oh, I don't know.

LICCY. Ça suffit!

HALLIE. All a bit above my –

ROALD. Nothing at all?

HALLIE. Um.

LICCY. She doesn't have to know.

ROALD. Israel still on your travel list?

LICCY. Haven't we had enough?

HALLIE. We're not going to the Middle East, so –

ROALD. But if you were?

LICCY. Why don't you just – [*go to the kitchen*]?

ROALD. Would you visit Israel?

LICCY (*to* ROALD). Let her get on.

ROALD. I'm just *curious*. After all you've heard.

LICCY. Heaven's sake.

ROALD (*to* HALLIE). Would you buy an Israeli avocado?

HALLIE. Oh, I don't –

ROALD. Or... would *refusing* to buy it be 'antisemitic'?

HALLIE *looks apprehensive*.

Simple question.

HALLIE. Does the avocado know it's Israeli?

ROALD. What?

HALLIE. Does it. Know?

ROALD. Christ.

HALLIE. Someone's got to stand with the avocados, Mr Dahl. That's all I'm saying.

ROALD *looks at her a moment, disappointed*.

ROALD. Go on, shoo.

HALLIE *scoots into the kitchen*. LICCY *lights her cigarette*.

Tough discovery.

LICCY. What?

ROALD. That your elderly fiancé is a Nazi.

LICCY. You're not elderly.

ROALD. Tom, if I am a goose-stepper, do I need to pay subs?

LICCY. My god, shut up.

ROALD. Get a membership card?

LICCY. Really. Everyone needs to. Shut up.

JESSIE *enters from the garden. A moment*.

ROALD. Ah. The dragon returns.

Beat.

JESSIE. If you'd like me to leave, please say.

ROALD. Have some sorbet first.

JESSIE. No, no thank you.

ROALD. Come come. You've already spurned Hallie's lemonade. Only so much 'no' she can take.

JESSIE. I'm fine.

ROALD. Go on. Cool your fiery mouth with Hallie's frozen yum.

JESSIE relents. Sits. ROALD scoops a bit for her. She tastes, smiles politely.

JESSIE. Very nice.

ROALD. Mouth less flame-y?

JESSIE smiles, reaches for her wine glass.

Ah, ah, ah, no more wine, I'm afraid, Mrs Stone. All for me now.

ROALD *picks his up, sips.*

Antisemites only.

Watches her a moment.

JESSIE. I think maybe I'd –

ROALD. Oh. Meant to ask. Have you actually *read* the book that I reviewed?

JESSIE. Um. Yes.

ROALD (*pleased*). Oh. (*To* JESSIE.) Doubt Tom has. He doesn't read, you know. Little Oompas at work hand him reports. Terrific with pictures – the best – but words – so *boooooooring.*

TOM. What are you doing?

ROALD (*to* TOM). You saw the photographs, darling?

TOM. Yes.

ROALD (*to* JESSIE). You?

JESSIE. Yes.

ROALD. And?

JESSIE. Shocking.

TOM. Terrible.

ROALD. Well at least we all agree on something.

Pause. ROALD *drinks again.*

Which?

JESSIE. What?

ROALD. The photograph?

JESSIE. Oh. God. Um.

ROALD. Yes?

JESSIE. The young man without – on crutches – without his leg.

ROALD. Sohail. Yes. Playing football when a penetration bomb exploded by his school. The book says the only reason he lived was, seconds before impact, he scored. Must have been an absolute thumper because all his friends mobbed him, tousling his hair, cocooning him from the blast. Well, nearly. Great chunk of flying concrete scythed through the gaggle, took his leg clean off. Ripped from his thighbone. I know pain, I do, but this… his arterial blood must have sprayed everywhere like a rogue garden hose.

LICCY. Please!

ROALD. Would have died there and then had some eagle-eye not spotted him in the carnage, tied off the wound.

LICCY. Stop!

ROALD. It's just fact, Lis! And why is that image not enough, on its own, for you to demand a halt? And what's wrong with insisting Jewish people, whose country it surely is, say 'not in my name'? Surely it's your voice we need above all? You say I'm antisemitic but what about you? Would you think about Sohail differently if he were Jewish? Did you look at that photo and see what I saw?

JESSIE. I said it was – I *said* –

ROALD. You say 'oh it's awful', I know, I heard, but a 'but' always followed, always does – eventually – because when it comes to it, a Palestinian child – that boy – has to be less equal than an Israeli. *Has* to be. Your righteous anger, your ancient wounds you hawk like cheap linen –

JESSIE. *How dare you?!*

ROALD. – they don't make you wiser – they give you partial sight. You can't wish for them what you wish for your own. Can you? Which is what enabled you to take the land in the first place.

JESSIE. It was a vote. A *vote*.

ROALD. They laid claim. They manoeuvred. And they took. Not the Arab Jews, not the Ethiopians. The Ashkenazis. Your people. Because you see what you *need* to see. A sanctuary, not another's home. And then you sit here, in my home, as my publishers, insisting I bow to a public clamour, utterly blind to how despicably racist you are yourself.

Beat.

Lis?

LICCY. Yes?

ROALD. Opinion?

LICCY. Only that it's nice to watch you expertly calm things down.

ROALD. Tom, darling?

TOM. Stop with the darling.

ROALD. A single authentic thought on any of this?

TOM. I said it's awful.

ROALD. What is?

TOM. Maiming children.

ROALD. Bravo. So, remind me, because I've slightly lost the thread here – why am *I* apologising?

TOM. Because the noise isn't entirely hysterical.

ROALD. Because… I'm antisemitic?

TOM. Because some of the things you said were not good.

JESSIE. *Finally*.

TOM. Some things.

ROALD. Not good, antisemitic not good?

Beat. TOM *under pressure.*

Dahl's-a-Nazi not good? Tom?

TOM. Bad. But she doesn't understand.

JESSIE. No?

TOM. England's another planet. No Manhattan. When I started at school a boy asked me – he'd never met a Jew in his life – if he could see my horns. Another dropped a coin near me in the playground, I went to pick it up, 'haha Jew'. Devils, money-grubbers. Bogeymen, all that. But malicious? Hm. Mostly it's boys finding good sticks to whack each other with. Not nice, but neither was my aunt's wallpaper. You just ignore it. Roald, he was at Repton. In the twenties. Training camp for the colonies. Beat the boys hard so they beat the natives harder.

ROALD. Porta Vacat Culpa.

TOM. I can only imagine what was said about *anyone* who didn't fit the bill.

JESSIE. And this is what? A British exemption clause?

TOM. Sticks for whacking. A tale, not *real*. Roald's my friend. Because he's clever and fun and generous and compassionate. Angry with what's happening, but not…

ROALD. What?

ACT TWO 71

TOM. That.

ROALD. Bravo.

TOM. There's a difference.

Beat.

I wouldn't be friends with someone who –

ROALD. What?

TOM. *Fundamentally* hates me.

ROALD. So we're friends?

TOM. *Yes.*

Beat.

ROALD. You know at least Mrs Stone spoke her mind. Risked something.

TOM. What have I just done?

ROALD. Neatly dodged the vexing bit.

TOM. All pretty vexing.

ROALD. Much better that I'm just drunken uncle Roald on Christmas Day, spouting old playground slurs. Because if I do hate Jews – and you accept that, put up with being around me for – I don't know – business reasons, then, I suppose, that's not great. For you. If I'm an antisemite, then what are you, Tom? A house Jew, I suppose.

JESSIE. I'm sorry?

LICCY. What does that mean?

ROALD. A friendly one you don't have to worry about. (*To* TOM.) And that would really rankle, wouldn't it, Tom? Upset your very Tom-ness.

JESSIE (*quietly*). Could you try for a taxi, Mrs Dahl?

LICCY. I'm not his wife yet, Mrs Stone.

ROALD (*calls loudly into the garden*). Wally! Wally! Leave that there! No, *there*! Good man!

Pause. ROALD *lights his cigarette. An intense pull and puff.*

(*To* LICCY, *of* WALLY.) He's wearing his woollen suit again. He's going to keel over if he's not careful.

LICCY. Tell him to go home then.

ROALD. Won't listen. Stubborn as a bloody ox.

ROALD *steps back inside. Looks at them.*

TOM. Look – everyone's frazzled –

ROALD. Not me!

TOM. – let me know tomorrow what you want to do.

ROALD. I can tell you now.

TOM. We can handle whatever.

ROALD. And off he dodges. Goodbye, Mighty Spootlicker.

TOM. Thank you, Liccy, the house is going to be magnificent.

ROALD. That's it? Niceties and vroom-vroom?

TOM. What else is left to say?

ROALD. What you actually think?

TOM. Do it or don't.

LICCY. I'll see you to the door.

TOM (*to* LICCY). It's fine, really.

ROALD. It's code, Tom! Secret conflab in the hall.

TOM (*to* LICCY). Let's do something with Fay soon. The four of us.

ROALD. Oh yes, laaaaaarvly.

LICCY. In town, yes.

TOM. Or ours.

ROALD. Ooooh in town, laaaarvly. Or yours, yes. Ta-ta, Tom.

TOM. Bye.

ROALD. Tom won't pay, of course, he never does. Stingy sod.

TOM (*pushing through*). Mrs Stone.

ROALD. Ta-ta, house Jew.

TOM *whips round to face* ROALD.

TOM (*seething*). Will you stop fucking calling me that?

They face each other for a moment.

ROALD. You know what, Tom. I'll do it. Say something. But only on condition you do too.

TOM. Do what?

ROALD. Call up your friends at *The Times* or the *Mail* or wherever you want to dingle your dangle and ask for some space.

TOM. Why?

ROALD. To express your concerns. If I'm to grovel, Tom, someone else has to growl. And who better than someone they'll actually listen to. Write an op-ed.

TOM. About what?

ROALD. The siege. The massacres. You choose. Stand up, say 'no more'. As a British Jew. 'Not in my name.'

TOM. This is absolutely insane.

ROALD. Is it? It'll cut through better from you than an old antisemite like me. Call time on their fundraisers, the lobbying, the Friends of Israel breakfasts with the PM.

TOM. Both sides bloody lobby, Roald!

Beat.

ROALD. I need to know my publisher is on my side.

LICCY. He is, Roald.

ROALD. So back me publicly!

TOM. No one gives a crap what I think.

ROALD. You invented the fucking Booker Prize.

TOM. I can't parrot your arguments in a national paper.

ROALD. You can option them without charge.

TOM. Just because they're free doesn't make them true.

ROALD (*an opinion!*). Ah.

Beat.

Saw Stan Collard last week.

TOM. Yes?

ROALD. Lovely chat outside the gents at Sheekey's. He'd been lurking. Oh hello, Roald, blah blah blah, loved the last one, how's Tom doing, still a cunt?

TOM. Fascinating.

ROALD. Offered me terms at Random House you couldn't ever match.

TOM. Outside the loos.

ROALD. It's a dirty business.

TOM. Liccy, please? This is –

ROALD. Why must Liccy protect you?

TOM. Roald. *Random House* are the cunts.

ROALD. Back me – back the Palestinians –

TOM. For fuck's sake.

ROALD. – and Collard can take a walk.

TOM. This isn't one of your nasty little revenge yarns. Flash-bastard Jew publisher gets his comeuppance! I publish you, I don't get written in. Understand?!

ROALD *finds his pocket address book, puts on his glasses, thumbs through. Hums to himself.*

What are you doing?

ROALD *finds a number, picks up the phone, starts to dial.*

LICCY. What are you doing, Roald?

TOM. What's he doing?

ACT TWO   75

ROALD *listens, hums.*

ROALD. It's ringing.

TOM. Who are you ringing?

ROALD. *The Times.* (*Phone.*) Ah, hello – Samantha Lawton, please, editorial, yes...

TOM. He's joking?

LICCY. Must be.

ROALD *flicks on the speakerphone.*

SWITCHBOARD (*on speaker*). Who shall I say is calling?

LICCY. Christ.

ROALD (*into phone*)....yes yes, it's Tom Maschler's assistant at Jonathan Cape.

SWITCHBOARD (*on phone*). And what's it concerning?

TOM (*low*). I came here to help you.

ROALD (*into phone*). Mr Maschler writing a piece this week –

TOM. Hang up!

ROALD (*into phone*). – about Palestine, about those awful attacks –

TOM *snatches the receiver, slams it down. Beat.*

TOM. I was at *school* when Israel was founded. *School.* It had absolutely fuck-all to do with me. This has fuck-all to do with me.

ROALD. A life shaped by the Holocaust. All that horror. The new *country* it spawned. It has everything to do with you.

TOM. Every Jew who got out is a flag-waving Israeli? Sorry to disappoint. I don't pine for Jerusalem. Don't crave being in the majority. I prefer to live and work with people *un*like me. Not just prefer, *need*. The idea of shacking up with four million other Jews is – (*Shudders.*) difference is the adventure. And okay, yes, I'm more curious about what's happening in Israel than *Spain*. But that's because people like you pounce on its every action. And then challenge me about it at parties. As if I know. As if I'm the fucking ambassador. As if I need to make my position clear or maybe perhaps *leave*. The room, or the fucking country, it's hard to say. So, yes, I'm a little faster to read the headlines when Sharon goes marauding in Lebanon. And maybe a tiny bit prouder when Israel does something positive or useful or just not shitty. Do I mean 'proud'? Maybe just relieved. Relieved to have a little respite from righteous lefties for a week or so. So to question my moral character, my courage, my loyalty to you, because I don't publicly speak out, is to misunderstand who I am.

ROALD. Who are you?

TOM. Well, I suppose, in the end, I'm... Tom Maschler.

JESSIE. So, can I ask...

ROALD. The dragon stirs.

JESSIE. ...if this country turned against you for being Jewish, where would you go?

TOM. Provence.

ROALD. Ha!

JESSIE. And if there was no option but Israel, where then?

TOM. If the only escape from a burning building is a passing haytruck, would I jump in? Yes. Of course I fucking would. Fucking hideous parlour game. Really, what does it do, Mrs Stone? Prove I can't be trusted. By them? By the 'English'! Christ! I hate it. I am English! I am English! I am English! As English as you Roald or Liccy or the fucking policeman on the door!

Beat.

ROALD. So why are you pushing me for a statement, Tom?

TOM. Because there are people *unlike* me, who don't see it as I do. And, before anything else, we are here to protect your interests.

ROALD. Money, money.

TOM. Your *standing* then, the recognition you might –

LICCY (*intercepting*). Point made.

TOM. It needs making.

LICCY. And you've made it.

TOM. It's not just cash.

LICCY. Thank you.

TOM (*still pumped*). It's not just your books we're selling.

LICCY. Could you give us – ?

TOM. Really?

LICCY. Mrs Stone too.

TOM (*impatient*). I *have* to go.

LICCY. You go when she goes.

TOM. Well she goes now.

LICCY. You stay – (*Sotto.*) we press, we resolve.

TOM (*huffs*). I'm not her minder.

LICCY. That's been your mistake today.

TOM. Alright, alright. A moment. Christ! Mrs Stone.

TOM reluctantly heads out towards the garden, stops to let JESSIE go out ahead of him.

LICCY. Walk round the lawn. Bit toxic still.

TOM. Isn't it just?

ROALD smokes, watches his guests.

ROALD. Look at them. He doesn't know whether to hang her from the oak tree or hurl her into the pyracantha.

He stretches – winces in pain.

LICCY. Sit.

ROALD leans on doorframe, winces, does a funny stretch to relieve some pain.

Please, you're making it worse.

ROALD. Wally showed me this. Learnt it from a medic in the war.

Final stretch, final, pained groans. Beat.

What is it? What do you want to say?

LICCY. Don't push Tom away.

ROALD. He's tough as anything.

LICCY. He adores you.

ROALD. Really, Lis.

LICCY. Don't be an arse.

ROALD. He's my publisher, darling. It's not love, it's profit.

LICCY. Well he says different. He says bringing you and Quent together gave him so much joy.

ROALD. 'He says', does he?

LICCY. We talk, yes.

ROALD. He also walks upstairs unaided, I suppose. Touches his toes without screaming. I've heard that's what the ladies go for these days.

LICCY. Let's be calm.

ROALD. Fucks without painkillers.

LICCY. Oh my god.

ROALD. You would, wouldn't you?

LICCY. Really?

ROALD. Or perhaps you prefer rickety old metallic giants?

LICCY. That's certainly the evidence before us.

ROALD. Six laminectomies, sure, but boy, that intact foreskin!

Beat.

LICCY. He's been –

ROALD. Do I appal you?

LICCY. What?

ROALD. Do I appal you?

LICCY. You have your moments.

ROALD. But now – do I appal you now?

LICCY. I *love* you.

ROALD. You having second thoughts?

LICCY. I love you.

ROALD. But if I appal you, why do you love me?

LICCY. This is just one afternoon of many. This is just one afternoon.

She goes to him – a small, tender caress.

And this – all this work – it's about the many other afternoons we'll have together.

ROALD. What's going on?

LICCY. Tom's been lobbying the honours committee on your behalf.

ROALD. Christ.

LICCY. I asked him to help. He jumped at it.

ROALD. Utterly craven.

LICCY. Don't play holy buggers. You know how it goes. Posh friends write gushy letters.

ROALD. Because I am about to die?

LICCY. Don't be ridiculous.

ROALD (*suspicious*). You want me proper? Like one of your lot?

LICCY. It'll do you good, Roald. Same as everything else we're doing here.

ROALD. A knighthood's like knocking down partition walls? Putting my dartboard in the annexe?

LICCY. Clearing clutter, inside and out. And if it will do that, I want it for you.

ROALD. And if I don't?

LICCY. But you do! Non-stop! Moaning that the adult writers get knighted but never you. So let's get it. Now. Five books, five years. They have to consider you. They will. They are. And whatever's ill-at-ease in you, let's banish it. Have you focus on your *work*, your life here, with me. With *me*. And not these sapping frustrations.

Beat.

But the honours committee. It loathes controversy.

ROALD (*realising*). No no.

LICCY. It's a rub-along club, you know that!

ROALD. I'm not dancing before a committee of… the *influential*.

LICCY. It's not the Moulin Rouge, it's a Sunday bloody supplement.

ROALD. It's swinging nipple tassels, Lis. They want me, they ask.

LICCY. Once you've worked for it!

ROALD. *Begged* more like.

LICCY. Do the interview. It's not begging. It's managing. Being practical. Grown-up.

ROALD (*attacks*). What a disgrace. What an utter fucking disgrace. To go chasing it. Grown-up! Really. A lapse, Lis, a *real* lapse. I am *honourable*. And it's no fucking honour if *that's* the price.

He moves away from her. Sits. LICCY *stews. Long pause.*

LICCY. Why did you sneak off that morning?

ROALD. What? When?

LICCY. The morning you posted that review to the magazine. I *saw* you, creeping out the gate, manila envelope practically stuffed inside your jacket.

ROALD. What's this now?

LICCY. It was boiling, why were you even *wearing* a jacket? You were all – (*Mimes shifty.*) You looked like one of bloody Quent's drawings – all pointy knees and elbows –

ROALD. Christ, I have pointy elbows, I can't not have pointy elbows.

LICCY. I saw you, out the front window...

ROALD. You're imagining things.

LICCY. Is that what you used to say to Pat?

Beat.

I know what you look like when you're sneaking around. We spent the last eleven years doing it. So don't tell me what I saw, *please*. You had to whisk that review off to the letterbox without my seeing you go. You knew what it was, you knew what I'd do and you kept it from me.

ROALD. You know I don't need your approval for what I write?

LICCY. You bloody do if there's a chance it'll endanger us. Me. My girls. Hallie even. And you knew it would. We have a policeman on the door because of what you chose to write.

ROALD. Let's not do this now.

LICCY. That man threatened to slit our throats as we slept.

ROALD. He would never have come near the place. Will never.

LICCY. Because they're all cowards?

ROALD. Yes!

LICCY. Fine, send the officer home. Why do we need him here if you're so certain?

ROALD. It's protocol.

LICCY. You're scared.

ROALD. No no.

LICCY. You're terrified.

ROALD. Why *must* I be terrified? Liccy, I know *you're* scared and I'm sorry. But this snarling Jew doesn't bite.

LICCY. How do you know?! How do you *know*?!! How can they be so violent in Israel, so dangerous, but so hopeless if they're down the road? Where's the logic, Roald? Where's the logic?!

Beat.

I love you but if we get married –

ROALD. If – ?

LICCY. – I need you to understand –

ROALD. If – ?

LICCY. I can't – I won't – be Pat. Collateral damage when you decide to strike out. No sneaking, Roald. You have to talk to me.

A huge old man with massive ears and hands and a bulbous nose pops his head through from the garden – this is WALLY SAUNDERS (*6-foot-5, seventies*), *Roald's ancient handyman, thickset, with a rural Norfolk accent that's sometimes hard to decipher. He wears overalls over woollen trousers, a shirt with rolled-up sleeves revealing army tattoos, and carries pruning shears.*

WALLY. Sorry to disturb, Mr Dahl, sir –

ROALD. Come in, Wally.

LICCY (*to* WALLY). One second please, Mr Saunders.

Beat. ROALD *nods to him. He steps back out.*

Take their advice. Do the interview. Calm this down. And reap what you deserve.

A moment as this sinks in.

(*To* WALLY.) Sorry, Mr Saunders, come in.

WALLY *comes in again.*

WALLY. Mrs Crodslan. (*To* ROALD.) The mawther, yer guest woman. She's sat on the caravan steps.

ROALD. Right.

LICCY. Where's Mr Maschler?

WALLY. When they came out the 'ouse, there were finger-pointin' and 'allerin' and Mr Maschler stole off.

LICCY (*calls*). Hallie!

WALLY. Uh found 'er trudgin' through the rose beds. Not lookin' at nothin' 'cept her own tears.

ROALD. Ugh.

ROALD *goes and peeks out at the garden*. LICCY *follows*.

WALLY. I pulled 'er out. Bit of a fright. Plonked 'er safe.

ROALD. Look at her, Lis.

WALLY. Pracally slarverin' like she's sadly.

LICCY (*calls*). Hallie!

HALLIE (*calls*). Yes!

LICCY. You seen Mr Maschler?!

HALLIE (*calls*). Yes!

LICCY (*calls*). Where?

HALLIE (*off*). He's playing tennis!

HALLIE *pops her head in*.

In the drive.

ROALD. Christ!

LICCY. With who?

HALLIE. Constable Dunn.

ROALD. Tell him to stop stealing policemen.

LICCY. And no scarpering...

HALLIE. What's that – ?

ROALD (*explaining*). Fucking off! No sudden exits.

HALLIE. Okay!

HALLIE *disappears*.

LICCY (*of* JESSIE). I'll speak to her.

ROALD. No.

LICCY. She's a mess.

ROALD. Let her stew.

LICCY. On the grounds, still our guest.

ROALD. Leave her to sting.

But LICCY *heads out into the garden.*

Leave her, Lis!

But she's gone.

Fuck's sake.

WALLY, *caught a moment in the wake of this awkwardness. Then:*

WALLY. Drive's not for tennis.

ROALD. Rake it in the morning.

WALLY. What's goin' on? It's loik Bedlam s'aternoon.

ROALD. You knock off home now, Wall.

WALLY. Got tuh fix the pear tree. Came down in the wind.

ROALD. It's Saharan out there. Tomorrow.

Beat.

WALLY (*apprehensive*). That copper – he – he be here tomorra too?

ROALD. Maybe not *that* one.

HALLIE *pokes her head in.*

And?

HALLIE. He asked me to ask if *you'd* decided yet.

ROALD. Swine.

HALLIE. Message back?

ROALD. Cold disdain.

A distant Maschler-whoop.

And cheer for the constable.

HALLIE. It's not really a match but –

ROALD. Help him win.

HALLIE. Right-o.

She goes, another sporting whoop from outside. WALLY *watches him a moment.*

ROALD. Did you ever fight with Jews, Wally? In the war, the desert –

WALLY. Figh' wi' Jews?

ROALD. In your regiment, I mean? Were there Jewish servicemen?

WALLY. Oh! Um –

ROALD. Or down the legion? Meet any there?

WALLY. Um. I don't – Not sure. Not that I know of –

ROALD. Thought not.

Beat. ROALD *looks out into the garden.*

She's walking with her now. They're walking.

ROALD *watches them.*

This mawther – she's Jewish –

WALLY (*without side*). Is she? Oh right…

ROALD. – and she told me that they're all terribly brave, her people. But I don't remember. Not in my squadron. Not in yours clearly. Not after the war at all those reunions and whatnot. I don't remember meeting Jewish serviceman. Just don't.

WALLY. I don't know about much beyond what I… (*Trying to make sense.*) That why she's spittin' and blarin'?

ROALD. Says I made up stories. In the thing I wrote that made that mad chap call in the night. Apparently I have to apologise.

WALLY. To who?

ROALD. The world.

WALLY (*shocked*). Wha'? You're not are you tho?

ROALD. I don't know. They've been on at me all afternoon. I needed you here earlier to fend them off.

WALLY. Ha!

ROALD. Where were you?

WALLY. Pear tree blew down. Nearly back up now.

ROALD. Well that is a relief.

Beat.

WALLY. Even Mrs Crodslan?

ROALD. What about her?

WALLY. Even she want you to say sorry?

ROALD says nothing. An admission. He looks out to the garden.

Don't let yersel' be pushed about. I don't know much, but I do know tha'. If you'd listened to other people, yeah, would you have done 'alf the things you've done?

ROALD. No.

WALLY. Made that valve after little Theo's accident? When all the doctors thought they knew it all? Would you'a got Mrs O'Neal back on 'er feet?

ROALD. Definitely not. She'd still be a vegetable.

WALLY. Or written half them bonkers books?

ROALD. No.

WALLY. So why do differen' now?

ROALD. The new book's coming out, Wally, and – they're trying to get me some daft honour.

WALLY. An 'onour?

ROALD. A knighthood.

WALLY. Blas'.

ROALD. Yes.

Beat.

WALLY. The house might be a-changin', Mr Dahl, but you can't, can yuh? A's who y'are, ent ut? Don't need no title on yer to be impressed.

ROALD. No?

WALLY. No. Well… maybe a smidge. It'd suit yer.

ROALD. This ol' rogue?

WALLY. Would I have to say Sir Roald when we're larkin'?

ROALD. If I can say Sir Walter.

WALLY. Ha! But if there's a price, well… Tricksy. You never bent to no one afore. And 'at din't turn out bad, did it?

ROALD. Thank you, Wally.

WALLY. No side.

ROALD. You're kind.

WALLY. You know where I am, Mr Dahl. If you need me.

ROALD. Thank you, Wally.

He goes towards the garden exit.

WALLY. 'Aving tea at six, but any time after six-thirty, just call. I'll tell Phillis. She won't mind.

ROALD. Thank you.

WALLY *notices a box against the wall.*

WALLY. That box – the wooden one – that Olivia's things int'it?

ROALD. Yes.

WALLY. Her toys and tha'?

ROALD. Yes.

WALLY. I remember. Can't forget. Lovely little mawther she were.

ROALD. Yes.

Beat.

WALLY. Her birthday last week, weren't ut?

ROALD. It was.

WALLY. Twenty-eight?

ROALD. Yes.

WALLY. God. Twenty year gone already. Funny thing. Lovely thing. Think what she'd be tellin' you now.

ROALD. She'd be asking for her tea.

WALLY. Not what I meant. Meant if she hadn't. If she was still.

ROALD. Yes I know.

WALLY. Night, sir.

ROALD. Night.

WALLY heads into the garden. The phone rings. ROALD tenses, his shoulder aches. It rings and rings. He tries to stretch out but the pain worsens. HALLIE nips in.

HALLIE. Oh, you're in here. I thought –

It keeps ringing.

Shall I answer?

ROALD. Leave it.

It rings off. ROALD tenses in frustration, a wave of pain climaxing.

HALLIE. You okay?

ROALD. Yes yes. Tom still there?

HALLIE. Um. Yes. They're chatting.

The phone rings again.

ROALD. Bloody bugger.

HALLIE. Think it's that guy...?

ROALD. No no.

Beat.

HALLIE. Want me to – ?

ROALD. No no.

HALLIE. You sure?

ROALD. Yes yes.

It rings off.

HALLIE. People are so keen to talk to you, aren't they? What you say really matters. Must be strange.

ROALD. Why?

HALLIE. No one gives a shit what I think.

ROALD. How old are you, Hallie?

HALLIE. Um, twenty-six.

ROALD. Old enough to help me.

HALLIE. With what?

ROALD. This.

HALLIE. Oh no, not the avocados, Mr D.

ROALD. What do you think I should do?

HALLIE. No!

ROALD. Go on, I'm giving the briefest of shits.

HALLIE. No no.

ROALD. Don't dangle your desire to be asked, then play all coy.

HALLIE. It's *so* complicated.

ROALD. Always deflecting.

HALLIE. It is, and I'm not. Do you want your chocolate?

ROALD. You're leaving us in a month. Forget I'm your boss.

HALLIE. Don't think of you / as –

ROALD. What should I do? Say sorry?

HALLIE. It's red-tin time.

ROALD. What should I do?

HALLIE. I got some more Milky Ways.

ROALD. What should I do?

HALLIE. I don't know, Mr Dahl.

ROALD. Did your father not encourage your views?

HALLIE. What?!

ROALD. Were you told to be quiet? You heard the debate. So. What?

HALLIE. I can't –

ROALD. What?!

HALLIE. No.

ROALD. What? What? What?!

The phone rings again.

Go on then.

She answers.

HALLIE. Gipsy House?...

ROALD *goes to the door, half-listening to the call, to peek out into the drive at* TOM.

Who?... Oh? Right... No no he's not here right now. Can I take a message? Yep yep. From where? (*She scribbles.*) Great. No I'll – I'll get his secretary to call you back. Oh yes, your number, sorry. (*She writes.*) Okay thank you, bye. (*She puts the phone down.*) Mike Coren from the *New Statesman*.

ROALD *laughs.*

Newspaper?

ROALD. Magazine.

HALLIE. Important?

ROALD. Clever lefties. What did he want?

HALLIE. Comment.

ROALD. Vulture.

ACT TWO   91

HALLIE. He sounded nice.

ROALD. He's a journalist. They're trained to sound nice.

HALLIE. Really?

ROALD. Third call in five minutes. Currently celebrating his own tenacity. Nice? Or annoying?

HALLIE. Annoying.

ROALD. You're too nice. Be less nice.

ROALD gets up suddenly, a jolt of agitation, not quite sure where to put himself, or what to do. HALLIE suddenly spots something in the garden.

HALLIE (*awkward*). Sorry, excuse me, Mr Dahl.

She goes out into the garden.

ROALD. What...?

She returns, scanning the room.

What are you doing?

HALLIE. Oh, uh, just –

ROALD. What?

HALLIE. – looking for Mrs Stone's handbag.

ROALD. Why can't she look for her own handbag? Where is she?

HALLIE. Just outside.

ROALD. Well get her in.

HALLIE. She'd, you know, I think, prefer not to.

ROALD. Why? For heaven's sake...

ROALD moves to the garden exit and speaks to an unseen JESSIE outside:

Why are you hovering out there?

JESSIE (*off*). I thought I'd – / seemed best to –

ROALD. No need for Hallie to scratch about for your – Hallie!

HALLIE. Found it.

ROALD. Miss Stone, come in and take / it please.

HALLIE. It's alright, / Mr Dahl.

ROALD. Stay there, Hallie.

HALLIE stays, clutching the bag.

Please come and take it.

Finally, JESSIE *comes in, uncertainly.*

Chop-chop.

JESSIE *walks across to* HALLIE, *takes it.*

JESSIE. Thank you.

HALLIE. 'S okay.

JESSIE makes to go.

ROALD. No no, don't be silly, wait in here.

JESSIE. I'd really prefer to.

ROALD. Well I'd prefer you to stay where I can see you.

Beat.

HALLIE. Jim shouldn't be too long.

JESSIE. Okay thanks.

ROALD. You ordered a taxi?

HALLIE. Mrs Crosland asked me.

ROALD. Aided and abetted, she flees.

HALLIE (*to* JESSIE). Can I get you anything?

JESSIE. I'm okay.

Pause. HALLIE *lingers on the edge of the room.*

ROALD. I understand you've been squishing my roses.

JESSIE. Um –

ROALD. My groundsman said you strayed into the beds –

ACT TWO   93

JESSIE. Apologies.

ROALD. This afternoon's most devalued currency.

JESSIE. I'll wait outside, Mr Dahl. Stupid not to learn from the past.

ROALD. Don't you want me to sign your book?

JESSIE. I'm sorry?

ROALD. Didn't you want your boy's book squiggled?

JESSIE. You wanted to get to know me before… squiggling.

ROALD. Ah yes, and haven't we just?

She looks at him a second.

No need to rain on his parade.

JESSIE (*relents*). Yes. Sure. Thank you.

She extracts the book from her bag, walks to him, hands it over.

ROALD. You know, the groundsman – he's partly the inspiration for a certain other cracking children's story.

JESSIE. He's definitely big.

ROALD. And *extremely* friendly.

HALLIE (*diverting*). Mr Blake sort of fused you and him, didn't he?

ROALD. Two of the planet's biggest, friendliest people. But they come here to see him, you know. He pretends he hates it, the little tart.

JESSIE. Any witches lurking about?

ROALD. Only one currently. What would you like me to write?

JESSIE. Um –

ROALD. Archie – that's it, isn't it?

JESSIE. Yeah.

ROALD bends to clear space at the table.

ROALD (*stops*). Tell me, if I'm all these terrible things / to you –

JESSIE. Please, Mr Dahl, I'd prefer to just –

ROALD. – things I can't see in myself, can you no longer read my books to dear Archie? If it's in me, then surely it's in the books too? Even if it's inadvertent –

JESSIE. I don't know if *everything* you are the books are too.

Space cleared, he sits, uncomfortably.

Archie loves your books. I'd find it hard to explain why I'd stopped reading them. I love them. Whatever you might imagine.

ROALD. Yes?

JESSIE. They make me feel what I felt as a child.

ROALD. What was that?

JESSIE. Scared and enchanted and excited.

ROALD (*appreciating this*). Hm. *Hm.* All gone now?

JESSIE. I get scared from time to time.

ROALD. Yes.

ROALD *starts to inscribe the book. Quite a long message. She's about to put it straight in her bag when:*

Won't you read it?

She does. Her energy notably shifts. She smiles as she reads it. It moves her.

JESSIE (*touched*). Thank you.

ROALD. Not at all. Archie's Archie.

JESSIE. He is.

Pause.

ROALD. Was it a tumour?

JESSIE. Huh?

ROALD. Archie – how did he...?

ACT TWO 95

JESSIE. Oh. Uh. Yes. Born with a brain tumour.

ROALD. Posterior fossa?

JESSIE (*slightly surprised by his knowledge*).Yes. *Very* posterior.

ROALD. Ah.

JESSIE. I don't know why we're talking about this…

ROALD. Why not?

JESSIE. I'm just not used to –

ROALD. You must be missing him?

JESSIE. Yes a lot.

ROALD. Tough with work.

JESSIE. Yes.

ROALD. And when do you fly home?

JESSIE. Soon. Tomorrow, first thing.

ROALD. Reunited in a jiffy. Upside of a flying visit. Remember it with Theo. When he was a boy. With all of them but – leaving him was…

Pause.

Don't forget your spidey scribbles.

He points to her article, still on the table.

Our bins are rather full, you see. Might have to go in the cess pit.

She thinks a moment, then, unable to resist:

JESSIE. Mr Dahl, when you do speak to Roger, please say I'll be in on Monday to clear my desk.

ROALD. Oh! Big swing! (*To* HALLIE.) Hear that, Hal, but how to respond?

HALLIE. To what?

ROALD. Her bravura exit line! She's desperate to know if I'll get her sacked.

JESSIE. No.

ROALD. But too proud to ask.

JESSIE (*to* HALLIE). Would you wait for my car?

ROALD. Come come.

JESSIE. Leave her, Mr Dahl.

ROALD. I'm giving a shit. (*To* HALLIE.) What *should* I tell Mr Straus? / Tell me.

HALLIE. I really don't –

ROALD. Tell me!

JESSIE (*snaps*). Just leave her!!

A stunned silence. JESSIE *dismisses* HALLIE, *who goes out to the drive:*

You don't *actually* hold my future in your hands, you know.

ROALD. No?

JESSIE. Much as the thought excites you.

ROALD. Think Roger won't tear you limb from limb?

JESSIE. If he does, it won't get you the result you crave.

ROALD. Which is what? I don't want you working there, that's all.

JESSIE. No, you want me in anguish, Mr Dahl. Because you're a belligerent, nasty child. And these threats and cruelties… a child's. It's the gift of your work, but the curse of your life. Have me fired, and I'll get rehired by publishers who understand exactly what happened here. That a broken boy in giant's clothing picked the legs off another ant and set it on fire.

She picks up the article, folds it sharply, slots it precisely back into her bag. ROALD *watches, realisation dawning.*

ROALD. Where *are* my pencils, by the way?

JESSIE. Sorry?

ACT TWO 97

ROALD. My Dixon Ticonderogas?

JESSIE. Don't know, sir.

ROALD. I'm clean out, you see, can't write without them, and they take an age to ship. I asked Roger's secretary to have you bring five packets as a matter of extreme urgency.

JESSIE. I'm not a stationery mule, sir. I wasn't in New York.

ROALD. What?

Beat.

JESSIE. I was in London already. There was no heroic red-eye. Roger wanted you to feel more valued.

ROALD. Without the agony of paying for it.

JESSIE. A well-meant white lie, nothing more.

ROALD. Nasty cheapskate swindler.

JESSIE. He said you left Knopf when you felt undervalued.

ROALD. Ironically I left Knopf because a stupid girl there didn't ship me my pencils.

JESSIE (*laughs*). Ah.

ROALD. Ah, what?

JESSIE. I heard there was more to it.

ROALD. Yes, Alfred didn't fucking sack the cow.

JESSIE. Oh, I heard you were vile to them.

ROALD. I need pencils. To write.

JESSIE. Non-stop vile and *they* got rid of *you*.

ROALD. No pencils, no books.

JESSIE. Fired you by letter.

ROALD. No books, no jobs for lying little desk monkeys.

JESSIE. I heard their entire staff *cheered* when they heard the news.

Brief respite.

ROALD. Why were you here, then? Some boozy book fair?

JESSIE. Vacation.

ROALD. With hubsy?

JESSIE. Yes.

ROALD (*suddenly*). And Archie?

JESSIE. Yes. First time abroad.

A realisation.

ROALD. You just told me you were missing him back home.

JESSIE. You asked me and I –

ROALD. To protect some frivolous deceit. Your *disabled* son. Who briefed you?

JESSIE. What?

ROALD. About my family, my boy? That Roger too? Or Maschler?!

JESSIE. Mr Maschler's *aware* that –

ROALD. One thing if you'd done it alone.

JESSIE. I'm sorry?

ROALD. But this…

JESSIE. Roger wanted the best / for you.

ROALD. A grotesque little charade.

JESSIE. Mr Dahl, it makes no difference how I got here.

ROALD. To you! To *you*! *I* want honest brokers! What else is a fucking lie?

JESSIE. Nothing!

ROALD. Did *The New York Time*s really call?

JESSIE. I'm sorry?

ROALD. Taft even real?

JESSIE. What?!

ROALD. I want to see these fucking letters he wrote!

JESSIE. Mr Dahl, please.

ROALD. Whispering, plotting, lying. (*Mock-innocence.*) 'How dare you say we work in cahoots! We're individuals, we don't control things.' Yet here you are – hiding behind your brain-damaged son, lying to curry favour, making up story after story – and now – unmasked! A nasty little gang. A nasty little cabal of nasty fucking Jews!

JESSIE, speechless, sits slowly, shaking, clutching her bag. HALLIE enters, clocks the tension.

HALLIE. It's here.

ROALD. Where's Tom?

HALLIE. With Mrs Crosland, outside. Everything okay?

ROALD. Ask them to come in. And tell the driver to wait a moment longer.

She goes back out. ROALD smiles at JESSIE.

Blackheath on your itinerary?

JESSIE. Uh?

ROALD. Rare place south of the river, away from the tourist crush, flowers galore. Archie like flowers?

JESSIE. What are you going to do?

TOM's a bit sweaty, pumped. LICCY follows, spots JESSIE's expression.

TOM. You've nothing to fear from intruders. Copper's relentless.

ROALD. Good.

TOM. A *machine*.

ROALD. He win?

TOM. Nah.

LICCY. All okay?

ROALD (*to* LICCY). Yes yes. Actually, very jolly.

LICCY. Yes?

ROALD. Good chat.

LICCY. Oh good.

ROALD. Look, Tom, I've been talking with Mrs Stone and thinking about what I said to you and I'm dreadfully sorry. Heat of the moment, back to the wall. I mean I'm barely English myself! And Lis, she told me about your marvellous hustling and I'm very touched. Forgive me. Sincerely. And thank you.

TOM. Well. Of course. It's no less than you deserve.

ROALD. So listen, I'll do it. Speak to this journalist.

TOM. Yes?

ROALD. Yes. It's a good idea, the one question, really good.

LICCY. You're sure?

ROALD. Don't make me churn it over one second more.

LICCY. Oh *good*. Good! That's terrific.

LICCY smiles appreciatively to JESSIE.

TOM. Great. That's… You sure? Not a bloody wind-up?

ROALD. No! Christ. Deadly serious.

TOM. Great. I'll have the office fix it first thing.

ROALD. Excellent. *Mail on Sunday*, is it?

TOM. Yes.

ROALD. I'm sure she's tip-top.

Beat.

TOM. Well then, if you don't mind, I'm going to run.

LICCY. Glorious you came.

TOM *heads to the door.*

JESSIE (*quietly, to* ROALD). What are you doing?

ROALD. Lis, darling, moment's grace in here, clear my head.

LICCY. Yes, of course.

ACT TWO   101

TOM. We'll have the proof picked up on Wednesday.

ROALD. Terrific!

TOM. Come on, Mrs Stone.

LICCY (*to* ROALD). Need anything?

ROALD. Only quiet.

TOM (*chivvying*). Stone?

JESSIE (*quietly, to* ROALD). What are you going to do?

ROALD. Enjoy the absence of others.

LICCY. Right, chop-chop, publishers. Party bags in the hall.

HALLIE. Bye, Mrs Stone, Mr Maschler.

TOM. Yes, bye.

HALLIE. Safe home.

ROALD. Back with your boy in no time.

HALLIE *goes into the house and* LICCY *marshals out an unsettled* JESSIE.

They're gone. ROALD *alone.*

ROALD *goes to the door to the hall, looks out sneakily, waits for silence, then shuts the doors. He goes to the notepad by the phone, picks it up, sits, dials.*

Hello? Yes, this Mike?... Good, this is Roald Dahl... Yes. I'm returning your call... Good... Thank you, most kind... yes – look I don't have long, work beckons, but if we're brief I'm sure there's – (*Listens.*) yes yes uh-huh yes...

Unseen by him, the door opens silently, carefully. It's HALLIE, *with a box of chocolates in a red tin*

Well yes I can explain absolutely – perhaps I shouldn't have said *all* are cowards, bit naughty, but it came from my wartime experience... well, Palestine, Libya, Middle East mainly. We saw almost none of them in the armed forces then... Well yes, but that's different, that's America...

HALLIE *gently clears her throat.* ROALD *turns, sees her, smiles. She smiles back apologetically, offers the red tin of treats but he waves her stay.*

MIKE. Mr Dahl, are you still there?

ROALD. No still here.

She smiles and, mischievously, ROALD *leans across, turns on the speaker:*

MIKE (*on speaker*). Mr Dahl?

ROALD. Yes?

MIKE. Do you – ?

ROALD (*winks at* HALLIE). Very much present.

MIKE. My father's Jewish and he received medals fighting in the war –

ROALD. Well I'm sure –

MIKE. – and a more distant relative was decorated fighting for the Soviets, so –

ROALD (*still making silly faces for* HALLIE). – well I'm sure your father was a wonderful man –

MIKE. He was. Do you see how hard it is to –

ROALD. Where did he serve?

MIKE. Bomber Command.

ROALD. …ah yes, well that makes sense. Pencil-sharpening does take courage. Those little razor blades – quite the terror.

Pause. ROALD *makes a 'naughty me' smile to* HALLIE, *but she's less certain.*

MIKE. Are you – ?

ROALD. Am I?

MIKE. Is this – ?

ROALD. What?

Beat.

MIKE. Nothing, do go on.

ROALD. It's simply a matter of fact, of *record*, really, that the Jews were always – how does one say it? – submissive, always needed saving…

MIKE. I'm not submissive.

ROALD. Are you full-fat though, Mike?

MIKE. I'm sorry?

ROALD. You say your father's Jewish as if your mother isn't.

MIKE....

ROALD. Semi-skimmed. Not even milk, in truth. If Mother isn't. I mean if you and I were in a line moving towards what we knew were gas chambers I'd rather have a go at taking one of the guards with me – wouldn't you?

Beat. HALLIE *is now very uneasy.*

Wouldn't you, Mike?

MIKE (*barely keeping a lid*). Sorry, Mr Dahl, just making notes.

ROALD. Yes yes. Scribble away.

ROALD *looks at* HALLIE, *winks.*

I didn't dare say in the article, one must be so careful these days, but there is a trait in the Jewish character that provokes animosity. A kind of lack of generosity towards non-Jews. There is simply a sense –

MIKE *clears his throat in discomfort.*

Okay there, Mike?

MIKE. I'm sorry, but I've never seen my father be anything other than deeply caring to my mother –

ROALD. A tribal closeness, you know, a sticking together. You know they killed twenty-two thousand civilians when they bombed Beirut last year?

MIKE. But what's that got to do with my father?

ROALD. Very much hushed up in the papers.

MIKE. Right?

ROALD. And who owns the papers, Mike?

MIKE. This one isn't.

ROALD. *In the main.*

MIKE. I can think of several / which –

ROALD. A sense perhaps that their pain is the only pain worth mentioning. Do you know? When it comes to Israel's appalling behaviour, I do believe you see it all clearly – in Israel's powerful influence over – over the US treasury, if we must be frank. Over the presidency. At any and all costs. Except its own.

ROALD *glances up at a shocked* HALLIE, *as if in cahoots. She doesn't know what to do.*

MIKE. Mr Dahl?

ROALD. Yes, Mike?

MIKE. Would you like me to call back later?

ROALD. Busy later.

MIKE. Are you sure you want this to... be on the record?

ROALD. Stick it *on* a record.

MIKE. Right.

ROALD. *Top of the* bloody *Pops*.

Beat.

MIKE. So – would you say, Mr Dahl, given everything, you're –

ROALD. An antisemite?

MIKE. Yes.

ROALD. Certainly I'm anti-Israeli, no secret – but yes, I do now think I've also become antisemitic in as much as you get a Jewish person in another country like England supporting Zionism. So I used to think they were separate things – Israelis, Jews – but now, now I see... no matter what they say, it's the same bag: the clubbing together, the assertion of influence, the outraged defence: you're imagining things! It's in your heads! Then bam! Right there, running rings round us. I mean Hitler, I mean there's always a reason why anti-anything crops up anywhere; even a stinker like Hitler didn't just pick on them for no reason.

Beat. HALLIE *goes into the kitchen.*

MIKE. Okay.

Beat.

Okay. I've got plenty. Thanks for your time, Mr Dahl.

ROALD. No absolutely. When will you print?

MIKE. Soon as we can.

ROALD. Jolly good. I'll keep an eye out.

MIKE. Okay thanks. Thank you. Goodbye.

ROALD. Thank you. Yes, goodbye.

He puts the phone down. Long pause. LICCY *pokes her head round the door, sees he's awake.*

LICCY. You still want to be alone?

ROALD. No no, utterly restored.

She comes up to him, wraps her arms around his shoulders and gives him a little hug.

What was that for?

LICCY. Being a good sport. It took a while but we got there.

ROALD. Yes yes.

LICCY. Tom already has a plan for how we can use your interview for the honours committee. I'm sorry I didn't tell you.

ROALD. Sneaky bugger.

LICCY. Didn't want to raise hopes. And I knew you'd find the fawning unpleasant.

ROALD. It's just mucky.

LICCY. It's the way of things. No exceptions.

ROALD *nods.*

We do what we do.

ROALD. Doo-doo-doo.

She kisses him.

LICCY. Want something sweet?

ROALD. No no.

LICCY (*calls*). Hallie?

Nothing.

Where is she?

ROALD. She was just –

LICCY. Hallie!

ROALD. Mourning the departure of Mr M, no doubt. Waving to a long-disappeared sports car.

LICCY *dashes out to the hall to look.*

LICCY (*off*). Not in the drive.

ROALD. Smoking behind the wall?

LICCY. Nope. Strange.

ROALD. No idea.

LICCY. She never vanishes.

LICCY *comes back in.*

Right, well. Toute seule.

LICCY *starts to clear, swooping some plates off the table and into the kitchen.*

That poor mad American – strange state she was in.

ROALD. Blubbering?

LICCY. No, just a – don't know – a stare. Found it hard to know what to say.

ROALD. What *did* you say?

LICCY. Oh, told her she'll survive. We all do one way or another.

ROALD *pulls himself up, goes to the radio, turns it on – a horse race about to start.*

ROALD. Ah. Lovely.

ACT TWO 107

He sits back down, listens to the race start. LICCY *enters with a tray, starts to load up.*

LICCY (*of a wine glass*). You want this?

ROALD. Oh, yes.

LICCY *brings it over. He takes it, then pulls her into him.*

I'm going to take some painkillers later. Perhaps we can…?

LICCY. Which Romantic are you quoting from this time?

ROALD. Shelley. 'Ode to Your Bum-Bum'.

LICCY. Yes he has such a way…

She kisses him. The kiss lingers. She pulls away reluctantly, continues to clear, scoots back to the kitchen. The race hots up, whilst LICCY *rinses plates.* ROALD *gets up slowly, painfully, stretches out again. The commentary builds.* LICCY *comes back in.*

Roald? Roald?

Beat.

Roald?

He turns to her.

We should get married in the autumn.

ROALD. Yes.

LICCY. Winter latest.

ROALD. Yes.

Lights down.

End of play.

Acknowledgements

I never planned to write this play, or any play at all. I've directed plays for over twenty years and playwrights always seemed to me to do something I could support, bring to the stage, but definitely not do myself. So in 2018, with an idea for a play in mind, I went looking for a playwright who might bring it to life. I pitched the idea to Nick Hytner, whom I had worked for when he ran the National Theatre, hoping to pique his interest as a producer. Nick really liked it, then, despite knowing I hadn't written a play in my life, asked 'Why don't *you* write it?' A mere five years later, in December 2022, I finally sent him a first draft (well, a nineteenth draft, but the first worth sending) and, four days later, he replied: 'Would you mind if I attached myself to direct it?' These two questions (Oh, and a third: 'Have you thought about John Lithgow as Roald Dahl?') have entirely transformed my working life. For Nick's intuition, belief and two years of inspiring collaboration, both in developing the play, finding the right home for it, amassing an astonishing cast and team, and staging a superlative production – a colossal thank you.

Between Nick's questions, there was the joyous hell of actually working out how to write the thing. And no one supported my daily frustrations more, nor tangled more with this play's delicate and unsettling politics, nor debated and challenged the characters' choices or, in the proofing stages, tracked missing commas and erroneous facts more determinedly than my amazing wife (and in-house sub-editor) Amy. And no one offered more (free, often daily) calm, lucid dramaturgical brilliance and speed-dialled therapy from 2018 to now, than the brilliant playwright and even more brilliant friend Amy Rosenthal. Without the two Amys, this play would never ever in a million years have seen the light of day.

I didn't realise how much I'd need friends, a gang of writers and directors I'd worked with over the years, to get those critical early drafts over the line. To Samuel Adamson, Cordelia O'Neill, Ryan Craig, Adam Foulds and Dominic Dromgoole for their vital early belief, vastly insightful, generous, impactful notes and encouragement. (And to Sam again for one of the most affirming, thoughtful emails I'll ever receive.) And to my agent Katie Haines for sticking by me through it all, for somehow having the play's journey all mapped out like a latter-day Nostradamus, and for pulling levers and strings at every possible juncture.

This is a play inspired by real people and by my interviews with those who interviewed, knew and worked with them. Immense thanks then to Angela Levin, David Godwin, the Reverend Michael Coren and Ann Thwaite for their time, memories and generosity. And my enormous debt and gratitude to all the brilliant biographers and writers who have made Roald Dahl their subject, especially Donald Sturrock and Jeremy Treglown, whose deep research and vivid prose provided me with so much detail and insight. Also to Piers Torday for his insights into the world of children's fiction and novel proofing and Robin Desser for her vital insights into the mechanics of the US publishing world. To the authenticity cops: Carl Prekopp for the Bishy Barnabees (in-joke) and the brilliant Anna Ziegler for her speedy New York dialect check-up. And to my researcher Fiorella Le Coutteaux for her speed and clarity and rigour. All that is accurate in the play is a result of their testimonies and work. Any inaccuracies and flights of fancy are on me.

When Nick Hytner decided to direct the play, we did a workshop. So thank you to the exceptional talents of Lydia Wilson, Helena Wilson and Hattie Morahan for their sharp contributions in the summer of 2023. And to the actors in the final show – Elliot, Richard, John, Tessa, Romola, Rachael – for the courage to take on this play at such a delicate time and for questioning, challenging, slashing, snipping, cutting, enriching and humanising every word on every page. And, again, to the truly marvellous John Lithgow for saying a delightful yes from the get-go and putting wind in all our sails.

There were two theatres involved in this production. The Bridge Theatre who initially developed the play – a huge thanks then to their team and especially to Will Mortimer, the Bridge's head of play development, for his early support and many excellent provocations. And of course, the Royal Court. Chapeau to Gillian Greer, the Court's Associate Dramaturg, for the epic script meets (me wittering, her patiently probing) and for pushing me yet further (and further!) when I thought I'd already arrived.

And to David Byrne, the Court's new boss, for his instant belief, his courage to programme *Giant* at a moment when others could have paused for thought, and for his unstinting kindness, wisdom and encouragement. And to everyone else at the Court who has welcomed this play in a way I could scarcely have dreamed of. I won't list names for fear of omissions and the subsequent social anxiety.

To Brian Lee and Dayna Bloom and their wonderful partners for their constant championing. Thanks also to Matt Applewhite, Sarah Liisa Wilkinson and the team at NHB for making this lovely book.

To my parents, Harvey and Linda, for everything. And to my glorious little boys (sorry, big boys) Remy and Lev, the next generation of avid Roald Dahl readers.

M.R.

Sources

The following publications are directly quoted in *Giant*:

Roald Dahl's review of Tony Clifton and Catherine Leroy's book *God Cried*, published in the *Literary Review* magazine on 1 August 1983, under the title 'Not a Chivalrous Affair'.

A phrase from Paul Johnson's opinion piece 'An Affront to Decency' which appeared in *The Spectator* on 3 September 1983. The phrase from paragraph one of the article '…the most disgraceful item to appear in a respectable British publication for a very long time' is twice (mis)quoted in the play.

Mike Coren's article 'Tale of the Unexpected', published in the *New Statesman*, 26 August 1983.

'Roald and the promiscuous girl', The Bryan Appleyard Interview, *The Independent*, 21 March 1990.

'My fateful interview with Roald Dahl brought me face to face with anti-Semitism', *Globe & Mail* (Toronto), by Michael Coren, published in December 2020.

www.nickhernbooks.co.uk

@nickhernbooks